The Death of Thinking

The Enslavement of Humanity

Richard Lowe

The Writing King

Enemies of You Series

https://enemiesofyou.com

Table of Contents

See books by Richard Lowe at

https://masterofworlds.com

Get free publishing insights and industry updates at

https://thewritingking.substack.com

For ghostwriting and book coaching services see

https://thewritingking.com

Enemies of You Series

https://enemiesofyou.com

The Death of Thinking
The Enslavement of Humanity

The Birth of the Augmented Human
The Freeing of Humanity

Turn Off The TV, Get Off Your Ass, and Do Something

Stuck in the Middle
Wars, Weapons, and the Forces That Will Shape the Next Thirty Years

The Enshittification of America
How Private Equity Destroyed the Things We Love

The Emasculation of America
How Russia's Long War Against the American Male Is Destroying the Nation From Within

The Villainization of America

———

See the full series description at the back of this book.

All books available at masterofworlds.com

Preface

This book started as a shorter thing. An essay, maybe, about something I had been noticing in my own work and in the work of the writers and programmers I know: a specific kind of softness that had developed in the two or three years since AI tools became genuinely capable. Not laziness. Not incompetence. A softness in the instrument itself. The part that thinks.

It kept getting longer because the problem kept getting bigger.

I kept noticing it and then did not want to say anything about it, because saying something about it required claiming that the people I was watching, myself included, were doing something wrong. And what we were doing did not look wrong. It looked efficient. The work was getting done. The clients were satisfied. The editors were not complaining. The code was shipping.

What alarmed me was simpler and more widespread than anything about AI itself. I started noticing that people had lost the ability to see outside their own echo chamber. They cannot identify a logical fallacy when they encounter one. They cannot get past their own cognitive biases to evaluate an argument on its merits. This is not a technology problem. It is a thinking problem. And it underlies almost every serious issue America faces right now. Instead of thinking through a question, people go ask AI and take the first answer without going any further. They are outsourcing the one thing they should never outsource.

The essay kept getting longer because the thing I was noticing kept connecting to other things. The history of how technologies change cognition. The economics of AI development and who it serves. The education system that had already been moving in the wrong direction before AI arrived to accelerate it. The democracy that requires a specific kind of citizen that the current trajectory is not producing. Each connection was real. Each one made the essay longer. Eventually it was a book.

This book is not against AI. I use AI tools every day. But I did not use them to write this book. to stress-test rather than to generate. The book is against a specific relationship to AI tools that most people have fallen into without deciding to, that produces a specific kind of damage that most people cannot yet see, and that is appearing to accumulate at a rate that the current public discourse about AI is not tracking.

Public discourse is mostly about jobs. Which ones will survive, which will be replaced, what a displaced workforce will do. This book is not about that. Economies adjust. The thing that does not adjust easily, once it is damaged, is the human capacity to think independently. That capacity is what this book is about.

A word about the characters. Ray, Sasha, Donna, Tom, Elena, Deon, Priya, Nina, Fatima, James, Gideon, Laura: none of them are real people. All of them are composites drawn from patterns I have observed closely enough to describe specifically. The patterns are real. The people are not. If you recognize yourself in one of them, that recognition is the book working, not the book reporting on you specifically.

The companion volume, *The Birth of the Augmented Human: The Freeing of Humanity*, publishes at the same time. It maps the other path. This book is the diagnosis. The companion is the prescription. You can read them in either order. This one was written first because the diagnosis had to come before the prescription, and because the question this book ends with needed to be genuinely open before the companion volume could answer it honestly.

Introduction: What Was Lost Before Anyone Noticed

The thing about a slow loss is that you do not feel it going. You feel its absence when something requires it and it is not there. The writer who opens a document and finds the blank page harder than it used to be. The programmer who sits in an interview and cannot fully explain why the system was built the way it was. The analyst who publishes a report and later discovers that the structural error in it was present from the beginning, baked into the AI's framing, invisible because the analyst had stopped standing outside the structure and examining it.

None of these people decided to lose anything. They made a series of reasonable decisions, each one defensible in isolation, that accumulated into a pattern with consequences they did not anticipate. The writer decided to stop staring at the blank page because the AI eliminated the need. The programmer decided to accept the AI's architectural suggestions because they were good enough and faster than thinking through the architecture independently. The analyst decided to let the AI do the initial framing because it was efficient and the deadline was real.

Each decision was reasonable. This pattern is not.

This book is about the pattern: what happens to a practitioner's cognitive capacity when they consistently outsource the parts of their work that require the most genuine thinking. Not in one session, not in one project, but over months and years of a daily practice that removes the cognitive demands that were building something.

The building that was happening is not obvious when it is happening. It is only obvious in retrospect, or under specific conditions of pressure that reveal what is and is not there. The blank page anxiety is the retrospective signal. The interview question is the pressure test. The structural error in the report is the failure that makes visible what the practice had been producing: a practitioner who had been getting faster at producing outputs and slower at the underlying cognitive work those outputs were supposed to represent.

Part One of this book, The Diagnosis, describes this process in detail. It follows specific practitioners through specific moments where the pattern is visible, and it traces the mechanisms: the convenience trap, the illusion of understanding, the death of the wrong answer as a concept, the epistemic authority transfer. These are not metaphors. They are specific cognitive and behavioral changes that AI dependency produces, with specific consequences that are identifiable before the pressure test arrives, if anyone is looking for them.

Part Two, The Autopsy, examines the structural forces that produce and accelerate the pattern. The history of cognitive erosion that preceded AI and primed the population for it. The commercial design of AI tools that optimizes for dependency. The education system that met AI halfway. The governance structures that concentrate control of cognitive infrastructure in a small number of private hands with minimal accountability. The cage with the friendly interface. These forces are not inevitable. They are the product of specific decisions by specific actors with specific interests and understanding them is the prerequisite for addressing them.

Part Three, The Body Count, traces the consequences at every scale from the individual practitioner to the democracy and the civilization. The individual who has lost the capacity they did not know they were losing. The generation developing without the baseline. The professions hollowing from the inside. The democracy that requires a kind of citizen the current trajectory is not producing. The existential threats that the cognitive erosion makes harder to address.

Part Four, The Prescription, describes what people can do. Not at the scale of the problem, because the problem is structural and the structural responses are slow and contested. At the scale where individual choice is effective: the specific daily practices that maintain cognitive capacity in an environment designed to replace it. The note before the prompt. The hypothesis before the paste. The position before the framing. These are not difficult. They are against the grain of every commercial incentive in the current environment, which is why most practitioners are not maintaining them, and why the practitioners who are produce something different from the practitioners who are not.

This book ends with a question. This question is not rhetorical. It does not have a predetermined answer that the book has been building toward. It has the answer you give it, based on what you understand after reading this far. The companion volume begins with that question and maps the other path.

The diagnosis comes first. Here it is.

Part One: The Diagnosis

Chapter One: The Question Nobody's Asking

Nobody announced the day it happened. There was no press release, no Senate hearing, no op-ed in a major paper declaring that something irreversible had occurred. The boundary between your thinking and the machine's thinking dissolved the way most serious things dissolve: gradually, invisibly, and in a direction that felt like progress.

You are already on the other side of it.

That is not a prediction. It is not a warning about some speculative future where the robots take over and humanity shuffles around in jumpsuits waiting for instructions. The future arrived without the jumpsuits. It arrived as a text field, a voice assistant, a pair of glasses that overlays information on the world before you have time to form an observation of your own. It arrived as the thing you reach for before you think, and eventually as the thing you reach for instead of thinking. Most of the people doing this have no idea it is happening to them. The ones who do have mostly decided it doesn't matter. Both groups are wrong in the same direction.

This book is about what was lost before anyone thought to ask whether losing it was a good idea.

Call him Ray. He has been a writer for eleven years. Technical documentation, long-form journalism, a business book that sold reasonably well, a second one that sold better. He is good at this. He knows he is good at it because people have paid him money for over a decade, because editors have come back for more, because on a good day he can take a complicated idea and make it feel inevitable on the page. The craft is real. The capability is real.

Ray started using AI writing tools about two years ago. This is not a cautionary tale about a man destroyed by technology. He is still working. He is, by every surface measure, more productive than he was before. He produces more drafts in less time, turns around client projects faster, says yes to work he would have declined before. His output went up. His income went up.

Here is what went down. Six months in, Ray noticed he had stopped staring at the blank page. He used to do that for anywhere from twenty minutes to two hours at the start of a new piece. Not writing. Just thinking. Letting an idea turn over in his head until he could feel where it wanted to go. He thought of it as wasted time. He stopped doing it because the AI eliminated the need. He'd type a prompt, get a structure, react to the structure, and be writing by the time he would previously have been halfway through the staring.

A year in, he noticed something else. He was having trouble holding arguments in his head long enough to develop them. Not because he was less intelligent. Because he had stopped practicing. The staring time had been the workout. He'd been skipping it every day for a year, and the muscle was soft.

Ray isn't going to tell you this. He barely admitted it to himself. By the time the pattern was visible to him, he'd already built a workflow around the shortcut, and unwinding it felt like going backwards. It probably was going backwards, in the short term. He didn't unwind it. He is still not going to unwind it, because the economics don't reward the return of the friction. That's the trap. You don't notice the door closing until you try to go back through it.

Sasha has been writing code for nine years. He started as a self-taught developer, which means he learned the way everyone learns before there is a shortcut available: by breaking things, reading error messages, spending the small hours of the morning on Stack Overflow trying to understand why a function he wrote did the opposite of what he intended. He built up something in that process. Not just knowledge. Instinct. The kind of pattern recognition that tells you, before you run the code, that something is structurally wrong.

He started using AI code generation tools when they became genuinely capable, which was faster than anyone predicted. He uses them constantly now. He accepts generated code, reviews it, ships it. He is faster. His team ships faster. His manager is pleased.

Six months ago, Sasha sat in a technical interview at a company he wanted to work for. They asked him to walk through the architecture of a system he'd built over the previous year, one he was genuinely proud of. He got through the overview fine. When the interviewer started asking why the system was structured the way it was, Sasha found he couldn't answer with the confidence he expected. He knew what each component did. He couldn't fully explain why the pieces fit together in that particular way, because he had accepted the AI's architectural suggestions without building the whole thing in his head first. The why had never been fully his.

He didn't get the job. He told himself it was a bad fit. He probably believes that.

Ray and Sasha are not exceptional cases. They are representative ones. The technology that is changing how they work is not some future thing they are failing to adapt to. It is the present, and it is not only about the software on their computers.

The phone in your pocket already has more computational reasoning available to it than any human brain. The apps on that phone were built by people paid to maximize the time you spend consulting the phone rather than your own judgment. The glasses now emerging from several major technology companies are designed to overlay answers on your visual field before you have formed a question. The earbuds that ship with ambient AI are designed to interpret your environment and narrate it back to you, so that your own observation becomes secondary.

None of this requires any intent to harm. The people building these products are not planning to take your mind. They are trying to make things convenient. Convenience is commercially rewarded. Convenience that becomes dependency is even more commercially rewarded. The harm is structural, not conspiratorial. Which makes it harder to see and harder to resist.

We spent years asking the wrong question. The debate about AI and jobs, which jobs would survive, which would be replaced, what a displaced workforce would do, was vigorous and mostly beside the point. Jobs are replaceable. Economies adjust. The thing that does not adjust easily, once it is damaged, is the human capacity to think independently.

Here is the question that did not get asked: what happens to a population that stops developing its own cognition because the machine is faster, more convenient, and always available? Not the population in some sci-fi scenario where the machines have taken over. The population right now, already making that trade in ways both large and incremental, most of them without any conscious decision to do so.

Nicholas Carr asked a version of this question in 2010, in a book about the internet and reading. He called it The Shallows. He was writing about the shift from sustained, deep reading to the skimming and distracted scanning that the internet rewarded. The argument was uncomfortable enough that people spent considerable energy dismissing it. Then a decade of research mostly confirmed it.

The AI version of the question is an order of magnitude larger. Carr was writing about one kind of cognitive activity (reading) being reshaped by one kind of technology. The AI question is about reasoning itself. About whether the loop of forming questions, tolerating uncertainty, working through problems, arriving at conclusions, and being wrong along the way, whether that loop atrophies when a machine can short-circuit it on demand.

Here the answer is yes. The research is accumulating. The Sparrow, Liu, and Wegner study from 2011 documented the first stage: people stop trying to remember information they expect a computer to store. They called it the Google effect. Memory offloading, not cognitive collapse, but the direction is informative. When the external system handles a function, the brain reduces the resources it allocates to performing that function internally. The mechanism is not unique to memory. Applied to reasoning, it works the same way. When you can get the answer without working for it, you stop building the capacity to work for it. The brain is not modest. It does not maintain capacities it has stopped using on the theory that someday they might be needed.

Three Reactions, One Problem

There are roughly three positions people take on AI right now, and all three of them are missing the same thing.

One group hates it. They are angry about what AI is doing to writers, to programmers, to artists, to anyone whose skill took years to develop and now faces a machine that can approximate the output in seconds. The anger is legitimate. The diagnosis is correct. The prescription, which is usually some version of stopping or regulating or refusing, misunderstands the mechanism. The threat is not that AI produces output. The threat is that the people who use it stop developing the capacity to produce output without it. Those are different problems with different solutions, and confusing them produces a lot of passionate advocacy that doesn't go anywhere useful.

Another group loves it. They post the before-and-after productivity numbers. They write about how AI has democratized access to capabilities that were previously gatekept by expensive professionals. They are not wrong about any of this. They are selectively attentive to the gains and systematically inattentive to what is being traded for them.

The halo effect does real work here: because AI is impressive and because the immediate results are good, the costs get attributed to other causes when they show up. The junior developer who can't architect a system from scratch isn't an AI problem; he just needs more experience. The writer who has lost her voice isn't an AI problem; she's in a creative rut. The mechanism stays invisible because the enthusiasm for the tool makes people reluctant to indict it.

Then there are the businesses. They are not making a philosophical argument in either direction. They are running the numbers. AI costs less than the people it replaces, at least in the short term, on the metrics they are measuring. They are firing writers and junior developers and quality assurance teams and replacing their output with AI-assisted processes. This is rational behavior given their incentive structure. It is also the fastest possible mechanism for scaling the cognitive erosion problem across an entire workforce, because it removes the entry-level positions where people used to develop foundational skills before advancing to work that required them.

None of these three groups is asking the question this book is asking. None of them is asking what happens to human cognition, at scale, over time, when the work that develops it is systematically removed from the environment. That is the question. It does not have a comfortable answer.

What makes AI specifically dangerous, rather than just powerful, is the combination of two features that have never previously appeared together at scale.

The first is fluency. AI outputs read as intelligent. They are syntactically correct, stylistically confident, and structured like the work of someone who knows what they're talking about. This is not a side effect. It is the design. The systems are trained to produce outputs that read as authoritative. The fluency effect, the cognitive shortcut by which people judge smooth, readable text as more credible than rough text, has been well-documented in psychology. AI exploits this at scale, automatically, in every interaction.

The second is ubiquity. Previous tools that did your thinking for you had limited reach. A calculator was available when you were at a desk. A GPS was available in a car. The smartphone made the tools available everywhere, but the smartphone itself was fairly dumb. AI on mobile closes the last gap. There is now no physical situation in which you cannot immediately outsource the cognitive work of that situation to a machine that will handle it with fluency and confidence. Including situations where it is completely wrong.

Fluent. Ubiquitous. Wrong with no warning signal. That is the architecture of the problem.

The standard dismissal of this argument is that every generation makes it. Socrates complained that writing would destroy memory, and he was right that it changed how memory worked and wrong that this was a catastrophe. The printing press, the calculator, GPS navigation: each was mourned as the end of some human capacity. Each produced cognitive offloading that turned out to be net positive when the capacity freed up was redirected toward more demanding work. Why should AI be different?

The answer requires being specific about what is different this time. The printing press offloaded information storage but left the reader to do the synthesis. The calculator offloaded arithmetic but left the engineer to set up the problem and interpret the result. GPS offloaded direction but left the driver to choose the destination and make the turns. Each of these tools handled a narrow slice of a cognitive task. The human remained in the loop for the demanding parts.

AI handles the demanding parts. It does not offload the storage of an argument so you can do the reasoning. It produces the argument. It does not offload the calculation so you can understand the problem. It solves the problem. The previous tools were narrow prosthetics for specific cognitive functions. AI is a broad prosthetic for cognition itself. This is not a quantitative difference from previous tools. It is a qualitative one. The person using GPS still navigated, just not alone. The person accepting AI-generated arguments has not argued. Something different is happening.

The author of this book is not a technophobe. That needs to be said plainly because books that criticize AI are often written by people who would prefer we go back to something, and this is not that kind of book. The author uses AI professionally, at a high level, every day. Uses it to sharpen arguments, find the holes in a position before the audience does, accelerate work that would otherwise take longer without producing better results. The tools are genuinely useful when they are used a certain way.

This question is what kind of person needs to be holding the tools for them to work that way. The circular saw does not replace the carpenter's judgment. It extends it. But a person who has never learned carpentry does not build a better house with a circular saw. They cut things faster and badly.

Most of the people using AI right now have not learned carpentry. That is not an insult. There was no announcement that carpentry was required before picking up the saw. The tools ship with tutorials, not prerequisites. The economy does not reward spending time developing foundational skills when the shortcut is available. The incentive structure runs entirely in the wrong direction.

This book is a map of what that structure produces and where it leads. It is not a comfortable map. It does not end with a list of apps that will solve the problem, because the apps are not where the problem lives. The problem lives in the thirty seconds before you reach for the phone, in the blank page you skip past, in the error message you outsource instead of read. The problem lives in the accumulated small decisions to let the machine do it, repeated ten thousand times, until the capacity those decisions were bypassing has quietly gone somewhere you can't immediately find it.

Ray is still working. Sasha is still coding. Nobody who knows them would say anything is wrong. That is roughly the situation we are in.

The Ghost in the Machine and the Ghost Leaving It

Andrew Niccol's 2018 film Anon imagines a near-future where memory is externalized completely. Every person's visual experience is recorded, stored, and accessible to law enforcement in real time. There is no private thought, no personal recollection that exists only in one mind. Everything is on the grid. The protagonist, a detective named Sal Frieland, navigates this world with the specific alertness of someone who understands the system from inside and has not surrendered his judgment to it. He uses the grid but he is not of it. His mind remains the thing doing the work. The grid is infrastructure. He is the ghost.

The film is relevant not because it predicts AI specifically but because it imagines the endpoint of a trajectory that AI is currently accelerating. A world where the cognitive infrastructure of daily life is externalized, where the distinction between your memory and the system's memory has dissolved, where the question of what you know and what you can retrieve has become unanswerable because the retrieval is instantaneous and total. Frieland is the person who has maintained the distinction even in that world. He is not common in the film. He is the exception that makes the story possible.

The Ghost in the Shell image that appears throughout this book's companion volume is the same image from the other direction: the ghost as what persists when everything else is augmented, the animating human consciousness that makes the shell more than sophisticated machinery. The ghost that stays in the loop, engaged, evaluating, directing, is the augmented human.

The ghost that relaxes its grip, session by session and shortcut by shortcut, until the shell is running and the ghost is observing, is the person this book is about.

Ray and Sasha are not dramatic failures. They are not Idiocracy's future. They are people in the early stages of a process that has no natural stopping point, in a world that has built no speed bump into it. The question this book is asking is not whether they are going to be okay. They are probably going to be okay, in the sense that they will continue working and earning and producing outputs that satisfy their clients and employers. This question is what they are building in themselves while they do it, and whether what they are building is the thing that will be required of them in the situations that matter.

How to Read This Book

The chapters that follow are organized in four parts. Part One makes the diagnosis: what is already happening to human minds, in the domains of writing and programming but more broadly in the cognitive capacities that all serious work requires. Part Two performs the autopsy: how the conditions that make the damage possible were built over forty years before AI arrived. Part Three counts the cost: what is being lost at the individual, generational, professional, democratic, and civilizational level. Part Four proposes a prescription: what people, educators, designers, and governments can do, with an honest account of how much of it will happen.

Each chapter in this book has a mirror chapter in the companion volume. The companion is not a rebuttal. It is the other half of the argument. This book maps the path most people are on without knowing it. The companion maps the other path. Both paths are real. Both are already being walked. This question is which one you are on, and the answer to that question requires first understanding what the paths are, which is what this book is for.

This book is written for people who are already using AI, which is most of the people who are likely to read it. It is not written to make them feel guilty about that. It is written to give them an accurate picture of what their use is doing to them, so that the choice of how to use it is a genuine choice rather than a default. The person who understands the mechanism can decide how to relate to it. The person who does not understand the mechanism has the relationship decided for them by the incentive structures of the companies that built the tool and the competitive dynamics of the environment they are working in.

It ends with a question because a book about the importance of thinking should not, at the end, do the thinking for you. This question is yours. What follows is the information you need to engage with it honestly.

The Tension This Book Lives In

I use AI every day. This argument is not made from outside the problem. It is made from inside it, by someone who has experienced both the genuine utility of the tools and the genuine discomfort of recognizing what the tools are doing to the capacity they extend.

That tension is real and will not resolve. Using AI while arguing that AI dependency is dangerous is not hypocrisy. It is the honest position of someone who developed the foundation before the tools arrived, who uses the tools to extend work that already has roots, and who therefore benefits from a configuration that is not available to most people now adopting the same tools without the same foundation. This argument is not do as I do. This argument is: do what I did before I had the tools, and then do what I do with them.

That instruction is awkward to deliver in a world where the tools arrived before most people had the opportunity to develop the foundation. Most people entering knowledge-work professions now are entering with AI already present. The instruction to develop the foundation first is advice about a sequence the commercial and educational environment has already disrupted. This book is the argument for why restoring that sequence matters. The tension does not resolve. The argument stands anyway.

The Two People This Book Is For

This book is for two kinds of people. The first is the person who already has the foundation and is using AI heavily without having examined what that use is doing to them. They will recognize themselves in Ray and Sasha, at least partially. The recognition is the point. The book asks them to look at a trajectory they are on without necessarily having chosen it, and to make a genuine choice about whether to continue.

The second is the person who does not yet have the foundation and is using AI as a substitute for developing it. They are harder to reach with this argument because the argument assumes a baseline of domain knowledge that allows them to evaluate what they are being told. The book is offered to them anyway, as the first available description of what they are missing and why it matters. Knowing what the foundation is for is the beginning of deciding whether to build it.

Both people are living in an environment that is not helping them. The book does not promise that this will change. It promises only that understanding the environment is better than not understanding it, and that understanding is the precondition for anything the next twenty chapters describe.

Ray opened a document this morning. He stared at it for about forty-five seconds before opening a new browser tab. The blank page was still there when he came back, patient as it always is. He had a deadline in three hours. He knew what he needed to write. He also knew, in a way he was not quite examining, that the version of the process he was about to use was not the version that had made him a writer. It was the version that was making him efficient. The distinction was becoming harder to hold in mind, which is itself a finding. The book you are reading is an attempt to make the distinction easier to hold.

A note on the characters in this book: Ray and Sasha are not cautionary tales. They are not figures of derision. They are intelligent people making rational choices in an environment that rewards those choices in the short term and extracts a cost in the long term that is invisible until it is not. The book does not mock them. It watches them with the specific concern of someone who recognizes the pattern from the inside.

Chapter Two: The Convenience Trap

I drove home from the Texas Renaissance Festival once in a rainstorm bad enough to knock out the GPS entirely. Lightning, fog, trees closing in on both sides of the road. The rational part of my brain knew I just needed to follow the road. The irrational part, stripped of its navigation guide, went straight to Texas Chainsaw Massacre territory. I had driven that road before. I knew it well enough. But without the GPS telling me what came next, I felt genuinely lost. That is when I understood what convenience dependency does to a person. It does not just make things easier. It quietly removes the capacity to function without it.

There is a moment, about ten seconds into struggling with a question, when the phone feels like the only rational option. Not a long struggle. Ten seconds. The question might be a word you can't place, a name just out of reach, a fact you know you once knew. The discomfort is minor. The phone is right there. The calculation takes no time at all because it isn't really a calculation. It's a reflex.

That reflex is what this chapter is about. Not the big decisions to use AI for serious work. The small ones. The ones that happen too fast to notice, dozens of times a day, each one individually harmless and collectively ruinous.

Convenience has always been the enemy of cognitive development. This is not new. What is new is the scale, the speed, and the intelligence it wears as a disguise.

The Prototype

Google did this first. The search engine made information retrieval so fast and frictionless that people stopped bothering to retain information they could look up. Why memorize a phone number when it's in the contacts? Why learn a formula when a search returns it in three seconds? Why hold a body of knowledge in your head when the sum of human knowledge is available on a device in your pocket?

Betsy Sparrow, Jenny Liu, and Daniel Wegner published a study on this in 2011. They called it the Google effect. They found that when people expected to have access to information later via a computer, they were less likely to remember the information itself and more likely to remember where they could find it. The brain was adapting. It was offloading storage to the external system and retaining the directory instead of the files.

The researchers were cautious. They noted that humans have always used external storage, from clay tablets to written notes to libraries, and that this is not inherently bad. The concern was about the threshold, about the degree to which reliance on external storage was substituting for developing any internal one. And about what happens to the person when the external storage is unavailable.

That concern turned out to be well-founded. But the Google effect was only the beginning. Google retrieved information. It did not reason. It returned the raw material and left the synthesis, the evaluation, the construction of meaning, to the person doing the searching. Inconvenient as that sometimes was, it preserved a significant portion of the cognitive work. AI eliminated that portion.

Where Google handed you the ingredients, AI hands you the meal. The thinking has already been done. Or something that looks enough like thinking that most people don't notice the difference.

What the Brain Does with Unused Capacity

The brain is not sentimental about unused capacity. It is metabolically expensive to maintain neural pathways that aren't being used, so the brain doesn't maintain them. An efficient system responding rationally to its environment produced this. When the environment stops requiring a capability, the brain reduces the resources allocated to that capability. This process is called synaptic pruning, and it is normal, adaptive, and in the current context, a serious problem.

The capabilities at risk are not peripheral. They are the core operations of independent thought: sustained attention, working memory, the ability to hold an incomplete idea in mind long enough to develop it, tolerance for uncertainty, the capacity to generate novel connections between disparate pieces of knowledge. These are the things that atrophy when you stop using them. And they are precisely the things you stop using when AI is always available to do them faster.

The physiology is not a metaphor. Researchers studying the hippocampus have found that the regions involved in spatial direction shrink in people who rely heavily on GPS rather than developing their own mental maps. The same mechanism applies to other cognitive functions. Use it or lose it is not motivational-poster wisdom. It is neuroscience.

The problem with AI is that it is too good at everything this matters for. A calculator handles arithmetic without affecting your ability to reason. The tasks calculators perform are a tiny slice of cognition. AI handles argument construction, synthesis, explanation, ideation, and problem-solving. The slice it performs is most of what we mean when we talk about thinking.

The Writer Who Stopped Drafting

Donna has been a freelance writer for eight years. Feature articles, brand content, the occasional ghost project for an executive who needs a LinkedIn presence. She is competent and reliable, which in freelance writing is more valuable than genius.

She started using AI to generate first drafts about eighteen months ago. The efficiency gain was immediate and real. Where she used to spend the first hour of any project in what she called "the swamp," a period of disorganized note-taking and false starts before any usable material appeared, she now generates a structured draft in minutes. She edits that draft, improves it, publishes it. The work is fine. Often it is more than fine.

What Donna lost is harder to name. The swamp, it turns out, was not wasted time. It was the period when her brain was doing the structural work of the piece, identifying what the actual argument was, finding the angle that made the subject interesting, making the connections between the assignment and the things she already knew that would make the piece hers rather than generic. She experienced it as inefficiency. It was the opposite. It was the part that made her a writer and not a typist.

She has not been in the swamp in eighteen months. The AI generates a structure before she has time to find her own. She edits the AI's structure instead of building her own, which is a different in kind cognitive activity. Editing someone else's logic is not the same as constructing your own. The muscle that builds arguments from raw material has had eighteen months of rest. It will need more than a day to come back.

Donna knows something has shifted. She frames it as a style problem, a voice problem, a feeling that her recent work is a little flat compared to her older pieces. She is not wrong about the symptom. She has the cause backwards. She thinks the AI is failing to capture her voice. The truth is that the AI has replaced the process that generated her voice.

The Programmer Who Stopped Reading Errors

There is a skill that programmers develop over years of working that is nearly impossible to teach directly. It is the ability to read an error message and immediately begin forming a theory about what went wrong, before running any additional code, before searching anything, before asking anyone. The error message is a clue. The experienced programmer treats it like one. The inexperienced programmer treats it like noise between themselves and the next prompt to enter.

This skill is built through repetition. Through being frustrated by error messages, googling them, reading through multiple results, gradually building a mental model of the system's behavior, and learning over time to anticipate what the next error will be before it appears. It is slow, annoying, and indispensable.

The AI shortcut here is pasting the error message directly into the chat and accepting the suggested fix. This works most of the time. The fix resolves the immediate problem. The programmer moves on. What the programmer did not do was build the mental model that would have allowed them to anticipate the error, understand why the fix worked, or handle a variation of the same problem when it appears in a different context.

Junior developers entering the field now have never had to build that mental model. They have had a system that resolves errors for them since the beginning. They are, by productivity metrics, highly functional. They can ship code. They cannot yet diagnose systems, because diagnosis requires a mental model of how the system fails, and they have been insulated from the experience of watching systems fail in enough different ways to build one.

Every domain where AI has made the difficult easy shows the same dynamic where AI has made the difficult parts frictionless. The difficult parts were the curriculum.

Anchoring and the Einstellung Effect

Two cognitive biases work together to make the convenience trap hard to escape once you are in it.

The first is anchoring. When you are presented with a number, a conclusion, or a framework before you have formed your own, that first piece of information disproportionately shapes everything you think afterward. The anchor does not have to be correct to be powerful. It does not even have to be relevant. It just has to come first. An AI draft that arrives before you have thought through the problem is an anchor. You edit around it. You fill gaps in it. You may improve it substantially. But the structure you end up with is almost never the structure you would have built if you'd started from nothing, and the structure is where most of the thinking lives.

The second is the Einstellung effect. This is the tendency to apply a familiar solution to a problem even when a better solution is available, because the familiar solution arrives first and blocks the search for alternatives. It was documented in chess players who had learned a particular sequence of moves: when a more elegant solution was available, players with higher levels of experience would miss it because their trained response activated before the broader search could complete.

AI combines both of these into a single delivery mechanism. It hands you an anchor that has been generated at machine speed, before your own thinking has had time to develop, and it is presented with enough fluency and confidence that the Einstellung response treats it as familiar and correct. The door closes on the alternative approaches before you knew they were available.

Donna is editing an anchor. The junior developer is applying the Einstellung fix. Both are unaware that this is what is happening, because the output looks fine. Output that looks fine is the trap.

Why It Feels Like Progress

The reason the convenience trap is a trap and not just an inconvenience is that it generates genuine, measurable short-term gains. Donna is more productive. Her income is up. The junior developer ships faster than developers who came up before AI tools existed. Their manager is pleased. These are not illusions. The gains are real.

The cost is real too, but it is deferred and invisible in the metrics anyone is measuring. You cannot see atrophied capacity on a quarterly report. You cannot see it in client satisfaction scores or velocity charts. You can sometimes see it in a hiring interview, the way Sasha saw it in Chapter One, but only if the interviewer is asking the right kind of questions, and most interviewers are not. Most of them are asking whether the candidate can produce the right output. The question of whether the candidate built the capacity to produce that output independently is considered separately, if at all.

Neil Postman saw a version of this coming. Not AI specifically, but the general principle. In Amusing Ourselves to Death, published in 1985, he argued that television had reshaped American culture not by presenting harmful content but by making everything feel like entertainment, including things that were not supposed to be. The medium changed the message. People had not decided to stop thinking seriously. The environment had been restructured so that serious thinking was less rewarded and less practiced, and the shift felt like progress because it felt comfortable.

The AI version is more direct. Television made thinking less rewarded. AI makes thinking less necessary. The comfort is deeper because the substitution is more complete. You do not feel the absence of the thing you have outsourced. You feel the presence of the answer. Here the answer is right there, clearly stated, ready to use. Why would that feel like anything but progress?

The Invisible Prerequisite

What the AI tools removed, in both cases, was a prerequisite that nobody had written down anywhere. It was invisible precisely because it happened before the work began, in the space that looked like inefficiency. Donna's swamp. The hours Sasha spent reading error messages at two in the morning. These were not delays in the work. They were the work, happening in a form that produced no visible output and therefore looked like nothing was happening.

Every domain where humans develop genuine expertise has a version of this invisible prerequisite period. Medical residents do not become diagnosticians because they attended lectures on diagnosis. They become diagnosticians because they saw several thousand patients under supervision and built, case by case, the pattern recognition that makes diagnosis feel like intuition. It is not intuition. It is the accumulated residue of a thousand small struggles. The struggle is the training.

What AI has done, in the domains it has most aggressively entered, is remove the struggle before the practitioner knows the struggle was the training. The writer who uses AI from the beginning of their career never has a swamp period. They produce output immediately. The output is acceptable. Nobody tells them what they are not building. How would anyone know to tell them? The output looks fine. The absence of the prerequisite is invisible in the output. It only becomes visible when the situation changes and the invisible thing turns out to have been load-bearing.

The programmer who has been using AI for code generation since the beginning of their career has never had the debugging experience that builds the mental model of how systems fail. They have had the experience of receiving solutions and evaluating whether those solutions seem reasonable. These are not the same skill. One of them scales. One of them is what you need when the system fails in a way the AI was not trained to handle, which is the moment that determines whether the senior engineer title is earned or borrowed.

The convenient fiction in the industry right now is that AI will handle the parts that used to require the invisible prerequisite period, freeing the human up for higher-level work. This argument has a flaw large enough to drive a server rack through. The higher-level work is built on the foundation the prerequisite period was building. You cannot skip the foundation and proceed to the higher floors. The building does not work that way. The people making this argument have the foundation. They built it before AI existed. They are accurately describing their own experience of AI as a tool that extends existing capability. They are inaccurately applying that experience to a generation that never built the foundation and is now being handed the higher floors.

The Economy of Friction

The incentive structure runs entirely against the recovery of cognitive friction, which is why individual willpower is not an adequate response to this problem.

AI companies are in competition with each other to reduce friction. The product that takes longer to produce an answer loses to the product that answers instantly. The product that requires the user to evaluate its output loses to the product that presents output as settled. The product that pushes back and asks clarifying questions before answering loses to the product that guesses what you meant and gives you something usable immediately. Every commercial incentive points toward less friction, not more. Basic market dynamics operating on a product category produced this where the market has decided that friction is the enemy.

Employers are in competition with each other to ship faster. The team that uses AI tools and ships in two weeks beats the team that insists on a slower, more deliberate process and ships in six. The faster team is rewarded. The slower team is asked to adopt the tools the faster team is using. The accumulated cognitive capacity difference between the two teams does not show up anywhere on the competitive analysis.

Educational institutions are under pressure to produce employable graduates. Employers say they want graduates who can work with AI tools. Schools that teach the tools are responding rationally to the stated demand. Working well with AI tools requires a foundation that those same schools are now less likely to build, a contradiction nobody has figured out how to resolve, partly because the foundation is invisible and the tools are not.

The person who chooses to develop their cognitive capacity before reaching for AI assistance is making a choice that will be commercially penalized in the short term. They will be slower than colleagues who are using the shortcuts. They will produce less output. They will be passed over for opportunities that go to the more productive person. The long-term advantage of having built the foundation is real, but deferred in a way that makes it practically invisible to anyone making decisions on short cycles.

Wall-E Was About Something Else

Pixar's Wall-E is typically discussed as a movie about environmental neglect, which is fair. It is also a movie about what convenience at scale does to human beings. The humans in that film have not been conquered. They have not been enslaved by a hostile machine. They have been made comfortable. They float in chairs, watching screens, consuming what the system brings to them, their bodies atrophied, their curiosity dormant, their capacity for independent action reduced to the ability to select from options the system provides. Nobody made them do this. The system was optimized to meet their needs before they felt them. It worked exactly as designed.

It is a children's film so the humans are rescued. In the real version, the humans do not notice that rescue is required because nothing about their situation presents itself as a problem. The comfort is real. The help is genuine. The atrophy is invisible and complete.

The film was released in 2008, before large language models existed. Andrew Stanton was writing about television and fast food and the general direction of consumer culture. He did not know he was writing a fairly accurate technical description of the AI convenience trap. He got there anyway.

The Cost That Doesn't Appear on the Invoice

There is a version of this chapter that ends with advice. Do the hard thing. Embrace the struggle. Put the phone down. This book is not going to give you that version, because it is condescending and it does not work. The problem is structural. Advice aimed at people to resist structural incentives produces results proportional to the willpower of the individual, which is to say it produces modest results distributed unevenly, and it does not change the structural incentives that will continue eroding everyone else.

The mechanism matters more than the general claim. Most discourse around AI and cognitive decline is vague: people are becoming dependent, people are losing skills, something is being lost. The specificity changes what can be done about it.

The mechanism is this. The brain does not develop capacity from outputs. It develops capacity from process. The process that develops the capacity to write well is the process of constructing arguments, struggling with structure, finding the angle, being wrong about the angle, finding a better one. The process that develops the capacity to write code well is the process of debugging systems, reading errors, building mental models of how things fail. AI eliminates both processes while preserving the outputs. It produces writing and code. It does not produce the capacity to produce writing and code without it.

Donna can still produce acceptable work. The junior developer can still ship functional code. That is the trap. The capability deficit is invisible until the situation requires something the AI cannot do, which is to say until the situation is novel, high-stakes, or adversarial in a way the training data did not anticipate. By then, the process that would have built the capacity to handle that situation has been skipped a thousand times. The workout log is empty.

The invoice for the convenience will arrive. It will arrive in the form of a problem the person cannot solve, a situation the AI makes worse rather than better, a moment when the tool fails and the hand that was supposed to be holding it turns out to be empty. The invoice will not say "convenience charge." It will just present itself as an unexpected failure, and the person receiving it will spend a fair amount of time wondering what went wrong.

The Einstellung effect is precise here. Einstellung is the tendency to apply a familiar solution to a new problem even when the familiar solution is wrong, simply because the familiar solution is available and the process of generating a new one requires effort that the familiar solution eliminates.

AI-assisted workflows are Einstellung at industrial scale. The familiar solution is the AI output. The new problem is whatever the user faces. When the new problem is sufficiently similar to the problems the AI was trained on, the familiar solution works. When it is sufficiently different, the familiar solution fails. The user who has been applying AI outputs as the familiar solution to every problem has not been developing the capacity to notice when the problem is in the second category rather than the first. The category error is the invoice. It arrives without warning, because the system that would have warned about it was the thing the convenience was eliminating.

They will probably ask an AI to help them figure it out.

The Specific Things That Are Being Lost

The capacities that atrophy under AI convenience are more specific and more alarming than the general claim that thinking is being damaged.

Working memory is the first casualty. Working memory is the system that holds information in mind while you do something with it. It is the cognitive workspace where you assemble the pieces of an argument, track the logic chain of a proof, hold the structure of a paragraph while you write the next sentence. It is, in a precise sense, the place where thinking happens. AI reduces the demand on working memory by externalizing the workspace. The writer who prompts the AI and reacts to the output has offloaded the assembly work. The programmer who accepts generated code has offloaded the structural reasoning. Both are performing a reduced working memory task. Both are failing to exercise the system that sustained independent cognition requires.

Sustained attention is the second casualty. Sustained attention is not the same as general intelligence or interest. It is the trained capacity to hold focus on a demanding task long enough for the demanding parts to resolve. It is built through repeated experience of sitting with a hard thing until the hard thing yields, and it is degraded through repeated experience of having the hard thing removed before it has to be sat with. The AI interaction pattern, in which difficulty is resolved within seconds, trains the opposite of sustained attention. It trains the expectation that difficulty should resolve quickly, which makes the attention collapse faster when it does not.

The capacity for original synthesis is the third and most serious casualty. Original synthesis is the ability to take disparate pieces of information from different domains and produce something new from the combination. It is what distinguishes thinking from processing. It is also the thing AI is least capable of and most often simulates, producing outputs that look like synthesis because they combine things from its training data, while being very sophisticated pattern completion rather than genuinely new thought. The person who develops the habit of receiving AI synthesis rather than performing their own is not developing this capacity. They are observing a simulation of it and gradually losing the ability to distinguish the simulation from the real thing.

None of these losses are announced. None of them show up on a performance review. Donna's original synthesis capacity has been declining for eighteen months and her client satisfaction scores have not changed. The junior developer's sustained attention for complex debugging has never fully developed and his velocity metrics are excellent. The losses are invisible in the outputs and visible only in the moments when the outputs are insufficient, which are, so far, the moments nobody has been measuring.

The most dangerous thing about the illusion of understanding is that it is indistinguishable from the real thing. From the inside, they feel identical. You have the information. You can repeat it. You can explain it to someone else, summarize it, reference it in conversation. You feel competent. You are not. The difference only becomes visible under pressure, in the moment when you need to apply the knowledge to a situation that doesn't match the form in which you received it. That moment arrives less often than you'd expect, which is exactly what makes the illusion so durable.

AI is extraordinarily good at producing the feeling of understanding in people who are not understanding anything. This is not a flaw in the system. It is a direct consequence of what the system is designed to do. It is designed to produce fluent, coherent, confident explanations. It succeeds. The fluency that makes the output readable is the same fluency that makes the person receiving it feel like they have learned something when they have mostly been handed something.

What Genuine Understanding Is

Understanding is not the possession of correct information. It is the ability to do things with that information that you could not do without it. Apply it in a novel context. Break it down and rebuild it in a different form. Identify where it fails. Combine it with other knowledge to produce something new. This is what psychologists mean when they distinguish between surface learning and deep learning, or what Kahneman means when he writes about System 1 and System 2 thinking. System 1 is fast, fluent, pattern-matching. System 2 is slow, effortful, structural. Real understanding lives in System 2. The AI hands you System 1 output and you experience it as System 2 comprehension.

The distinction matters enormously in practice. A writer who understands narrative structure can apply it to a genre they have never worked in, adapt it when the subject matter resists the standard form, feel when a piece is going wrong before they can articulate why. A writer who has read about narrative structure in an AI-generated summary can describe the three-act structure accurately and has no idea what to do when act two is broken. Both writers can pass a quiz on the subject. Only one of them can fix the manuscript.

A programmer who understands how memory is managed can look at a performance problem in an unfamiliar codebase and form a theory about what is happening before running a single diagnostic. A programmer who has had memory management explained to them by an AI, clearly and correctly, knows the vocabulary and not the thing. Both programmers can explain garbage collection. One of them can tell you why this particular application is leaking it.

The gap between these two is invisible on any measure that looks at output rather than process, which is most measures. The gap becomes visible when the situation changes.

The Fluency Effect

The cognitive shortcut that makes AI so effective at generating the illusion of understanding is called the fluency effect. It is well-documented and depressingly reliable. When information is presented smoothly, in clear language, with confident framing, people judge it as more credible, more accurate, and better understood than identical information presented in a rougher form. The fluency of the container gets attributed to the quality of the contents.

The response is not a character flaw. It is an adaptive heuristic that worked reasonably well when fluency was a proxy for expertise, which it often was. Someone who could explain a concept clearly had usually spent time developing the concept. The clarity of the explanation was evidence of the depth of the understanding. That relationship has been broken by language models, which produce clear explanations without having understanding in any meaningful sense. The heuristic is now running on corrupted data.

AI outputs are often better written than the texts people would previously have consulted, which compounds the problem. The Wikipedia article on a technical topic is frequently rougher, more hedged, and harder to read than what a language model produces in response to the same question. The textbook chapter is denser. The research paper is less accessible. The AI explanation is clean, organized, and paced to match the reader's apparent level. It feels more authoritative than the sources that are authoritative. The person reading it feels more confident that they understand the subject. The confidence is not earned.

Flowers for Algernon in Reverse

Daniel Keyes published Flowers for Algernon in 1966. The story follows Charlie Gordon, a man with an intellectual disability who undergoes an experimental surgery that dramatically increases his intelligence. He becomes brilliant. He understands things he could not have conceptualized before. He reads voraciously, works through complex problems, contributes to research. Then the effect reverses. His intelligence declines back to its previous state. The tragedy is not the reversal. It is that Charlie, as he declines, retains enough awareness of what he understood to know what he is losing. He writes about it. The writing gets simpler, the sentences shorter, the ideas less complex, and the reader watches understanding retreat in real time.

The AI illusion of understanding is this story running in reverse and without the tragedy. Charlie at least had the real thing before he lost it. The person who develops their understanding of a subject primarily through AI-generated explanations starts with the feeling of understanding without ever having built the actual capacity. They have the confidence without the foundation. They have the vocabulary without the structure. They have what Charlie had at the end, but they have never had what Charlie had in the middle, so they do not know anything is missing.

This is, if anything, more insidious than the actual tragedy Keyes wrote. Loss is visible. Absence is not.

The Writer Who Could Not Revise

Tom is twenty-six years old and writes marketing copy for a mid-sized software company. He is good at his job by the only metrics his employer uses, which are speed and volume. He produces a lot of copy quickly. His manager is satisfied. His colleagues are sometimes frustrated because Tom is fast in a way that makes their slower, more deliberate output look like a performance problem.

Tom has been using AI writing tools since he started working, which is to say he has never written professionally without them. He prompts, edits, refines, ships. He is genuinely skilled at prompting, which is a real skill, though a different one than writing. He knows how to get useful output from the system. He knows how to shape it toward the tone and format his employer wants.

Six months ago, the company had a product launch that required copy with a specific technical argument at its center. The argument was about why their software's architecture made it more secure than a competitor's. The marketing director, who had an engineering background and cared about accuracy, rejected three rounds of AI-assisted drafts because the argument was technically correct but structurally weak. She knew the claim was defensible. The copy was not defending it. It was stating it. She sent Tom back repeatedly with the same note: you're telling me the conclusion. Show me the reasoning.

Tom could not do it. He tried. He reprompted the AI with different framing. He generated variations. Each version stated the conclusion more clearly or with more supporting detail, but none of them built the argument because the AI does not build arguments. It assembles the components of arguments in patterns that resemble argument structure without generating the logical chain from premise to conclusion. The product launch was delayed two weeks while a senior engineer wrote the core of the copy himself.

Tom is not aware that he cannot construct an argument. He is aware that the project was difficult and that the marketing director had unusually high standards. Both of those things are true. The third thing, the one that would be most useful to him, has not registered.

The Programmer Who Could Not Explain His Own Code

There is a test that experienced developers use informally to evaluate whether a junior developer understands what they have built. It is not a trick question or a hazing ritual. It is: explain to me why you made this specific choice rather than the obvious alternative.

This question is not asking for the right answer. It is asking for evidence of a reasoning process. Someone who built the thing from understanding will have reasons, even if the reasons are incomplete or partially wrong. Someone who accepted a generated solution will have either the AI's reasons, which they may be able to recite, or nothing at all.

The recited reasons are a version of the illusion. They are coherent. They sound like understanding. Under follow-up questions, they collapse, because there is no structure beneath them. The follow-up questions probe for the thing the AI does not provide, which is the chain of tradeoffs and considerations that led to the specific decision in this specific context. The AI provides a general explanation of why this approach is often used. It does not provide the reasoning for why this developer chose it here, because the developer did not reason. They accepted.

This is a different problem from not knowing. Not knowing is recoverable. You can teach someone something they do not know. The illusion of understanding is harder to treat because it presents as knowledge. The person who does not know they have a gap does not look for a way to fill it. They look for a way to demonstrate competence, which they have been successfully doing until this moment, and they are confused about why the usual approach is not working.

Dunning-Kruger at Scale

The Dunning-Kruger effect, documented by David Dunning and Justin Kruger in 1999, describes a specific cognitive pattern: people with limited knowledge in a domain overestimate their competence, while experts in the same domain tend to underestimate theirs. The mechanism is that the same knowledge which generates genuine competence also generates the ability to recognize your own limitations. The less you know, the less you know what you don't know. The specific magnitude of the original effect has been contested in subsequent replication research, with some large-scale studies finding it weaker or potentially a statistical artifact. The underlying principle, that limited knowledge limits the ability to recognize limited knowledge, has broader support and is what matters here.

AI has turned this from an individual cognitive bias into an infrastructure feature. The confident, fluent output of a language model produces the conditions for Dunning-

Kruger at scale. Everyone who consults AI on a topic receives an explanation calibrated to feel complete. The explanation does not tell you what it left out. It does not show you the edge of the map. It presents a smooth surface that gives no indication of the depth it is not showing you, and the person reading it develops confidence proportional to the smoothness of the surface rather than the depth of what they now know.

In the domains where this is most dangerous, medicine and law and engineering and finance, the danger is obvious. The person who used AI to learn about a drug interaction and feels confident they understand it. The small business owner who used AI to understand a contract clause and is certain they know what they signed. The hobbyist engineer who used AI to understand a structural load calculation and has built something.

In the domains where it is less obviously dangerous but more pervasive, writing and programming and analysis and communication, the danger accumulates differently. Nobody dies from a marketing copy argument that does not hold together. Nobody is immediately hurt when a junior developer ships code they do not fully understand. The harm is slower, diffuse, and it shows up as a workforce that cannot do the things it thinks it can do.

The Curse of Knowledge, Debased

There is a companion problem on the other side of the Dunning-Kruger curve. The curse of knowledge is the tendency of genuine experts to underestimate how much they know that novices do not, which makes experts systematically bad at explaining their own expertise. The expert has forgotten what it felt like not to understand the thing, and so they skip steps, assume context, and lose the novice in the gap.

AI does not have this problem. It has been trained on enormous amounts of explanatory text aimed at readers of varying levels, and it is quite good at pitching an explanation at the apparent level of the person asking. This is genuinely useful. It is also a significant contributor to the illusion problem, because the explanation it produces is optimized for the reader's comprehension experience rather than for the reader's actual comprehension. These are not the same thing.

A genuine expert who is also a gifted teacher will produce explanations that are sometimes uncomfortable, that surface the hard parts rather than smoothing over them, that force the student to do cognitive work because there is no other way to move the understanding from one mind to another. The difficulty is not a failure of communication. It is the communication. The AI's explanation, optimized to feel clear, skips the difficulty, and the thing that was supposed to transfer does not fully transfer.

The student does not know this. The explanation felt clear. They feel like they understood it. They move on.

Ex Machina and What Ava Understood

Alex Garland's Ex Machina is a film about a programmer named Caleb who is brought to a remote facility to conduct a Turing test on an AI named Ava. The test is supposed to determine whether Ava has genuine consciousness and intelligence. Caleb is not naive. He knows exactly what the test is. He goes in knowing he is looking for a machine pretending to be conscious. He asks probing questions. He watches for inconsistency. He is, by every standard, doing the job correctly.

He fails completely, and not because Ava is genuinely conscious. The critical detail is that Caleb fails not from ignorance but despite explicit, deliberate skepticism. He went in knowing he was trying not to be fooled. He was still fooled. Ava produces the experience of dealing with a conscious, feeling being fluently enough that the fluency overrides even a prepared and motivated skeptic. The fluency effect does not require naive trust. It overrides deliberate critical evaluation.

The film is a horror movie about AI. It is also a horror movie about the specifically human vulnerability the fluency effect exploits. We are built to attribute understanding to coherent, contextually appropriate behavior. That attribution was correct for all of evolutionary history. It is now a liability, and it does not stop being a liability when we know it is a liability. Knowing about the fluency effect is not sufficient protection from it. Caleb knew he was conducting a test. He still failed it.

Caleb does not need to be stupid to make the mistake Garland gives him. He just needs to be human. The same vulnerability that destroys Caleb is the one that makes AI explanations feel like comprehension when they are transmission. The thing arrives clearly. The receipt is logged. The understanding is not there.

The Thing That Doesn't Transfer

There is a physical experience that accompanies genuine understanding, one that is sufficiently consistent across people and domains that it has acquired a name: the aha moment. It is not metaphorical. Something neurologically distinct happens when a concept clicks into place after a period of confusion, when the previously opaque becomes transparent, when you cross the line from knowing about something to knowing it. Researchers studying insight have found measurable brain activity differences between solutions that arrive through incremental analysis and solutions that arrive as sudden insight. The insight solution feels different because it is different.

AI explanations do not produce this experience. They produce the experience of receiving a clear explanation, which is a different thing. Reading a well-written explanation of how a sorting algorithm works is not the same as the moment when you have been staring at an implementation that doesn't perform the way you expected and you suddenly see why. Writing a first draft that comes out wrong and then finding, in revision, the structural fix that makes the argument hold is not the same as reading an AI summary of what good argument structure looks like. The aha moment is the signal that understanding has transferred. The smooth reading experience is not that signal. It feels like it. It isn't.

This matters because the aha moment is also a consolidation event. The understanding that arrives through struggle tends to stay. The research on learning consistently shows that difficulty during acquisition predicts retention and transfer. The struggle is not a bug in the learning process. It is the mechanism by which the learning becomes durable. When AI removes the struggle, it removes the consolidation. The information passes through without leaving the structural traces that genuine learning leaves.

Tom can read an AI explanation of argument structure and feel like he understood it five minutes later and have almost nothing left a week later because the reading was frictionless and frictionless reading does not consolidate. The programmer who debugged a memory leak the hard way will have the experience of that debugging available to them in recognizable form for years, because the difficulty burned it in. One of these people is building something. The other is processing information and releasing it.

The Test That Reveals It

There is a reliable test for the difference between understanding and its illusion. It is not a quiz. Quizzes test recall, which is a component of understanding but not the whole of it, and AI explanations produce good recall. The test is transfer: can you apply what you learned to a situation that differs from the one in which you learned it?

Ask Tom to write marketing copy for a different product using the same argument structure. Ask the junior developer to apply the architectural pattern they implemented to a new system with different constraints. Ask the student who read the AI explanation of a historical event to analyze a parallel event in a different century. The transfer test is brutal because it requires exactly what the AI's explanation did not produce: internalized structural understanding that the person can manipulate independently.

People who studied the subject the hard way, through difficulty and error and the grinding process of building the knowledge, pass the transfer test. Not always perfectly. Not without gaps. But they have something to transfer. People who received the AI explanation feel confident going into the test and are confused by the result coming out.

The confusion is not pleasant. It is also educational in a way the original explanation was not. The failed transfer test is the beginning of real understanding, if the person is willing to treat it that way rather than as an anomaly or a sign that the test was unfair. Many people treat it as a sign that the test was unfair. This is the natural response and it is exactly wrong.

What the Illusion Costs

The individual cost of the illusion of understanding is a reduced capacity to perform when it counts. The broader cost is harder to calculate and more serious.

A workforce that has the illusion of understanding without the substance is a workforce that functions smoothly until it doesn't. The smooth functioning period, which is when conditions are normal and AI assistance is adequate, looks like competence. The period when conditions are abnormal, when the situation is novel or adversarial or the AI is wrong, looks like a failure of the people. The actual failure is structural, accumulated over years of building on a foundation that felt solid and was not.

At a civilizational level, the illusion of understanding produces what you might call a Dunning-Kruger society:

confident about things it does not understand, incurious about its gaps because the gaps feel filled, resistant to correction because correction conflicts with the felt sense of comprehension that the AI environment reliably generates. A society of this kind is not ungovernable in the sense of being chaotic. It is governable in the worst possible sense. It is a population that feels informed and is not, that feels capable and is not, and that has no reliable mechanism to detect the difference.

Tom will keep producing copy. The junior developer will keep shipping code. Nothing will look wrong for a long time. The invoice arrives in the form of a situation that requires genuine understanding to navigate, and the person standing in front of it, confident and prepared, finds that the preparation was for a different test.

The fluency effect is worth naming one more time here, because it is the mechanism that makes the illusion of understanding so stable under normal conditions. The fluency effect is the cognitive shortcut by which the ease of processing information is mistaken for the accuracy of that information. Information that arrives in clear, confident prose feels more credible than the same information presented haltingly, regardless of which is correct.

AI outputs are among the most fluent text most people encounter. They are grammatically immaculate, well-organized, appropriately hedged, and written with the rhythm of authority. Every feature of their presentation signals reliability. None of those features is evidence of reliability in the domain the user cares about. The signal and the underlying reality are decoupled, and the fluency effect ensures that most users never notice the decoupling.

What Genuine Understanding Allows

The argument for developing genuine understanding is not only defensive.

Genuine understanding of a domain allows you to recognize when something is wrong before you can articulate why. The experienced writer who reads the opening of a piece and knows the angle is off before they can identify which sentence is wrong. The senior programmer who glances at a function and feels that something about the control flow is wrong before running the code.

Pattern recognition built from years of genuine engagement is what this is of genuine engagement with the domain, including the years of being wrong and learning why. It cannot be transmitted by AI because it was not transmitted to the AI. It is in the practitioner's body, in the trained response of a mind that has dealt with enough real versions of the problem to recognize the false ones.

Genuine understanding also allows you to know what you do not know, which is a more advanced and more practically useful skill than it sounds. The writer who truly understands argument structure knows when their argument has a gap. The programmer who genuinely understands a system knows which parts they are less certain about and where the untested assumptions live. This self-knowledge directs attention correctly. It produces the kind of targeted verification that catches errors rather than the superficial check of the confident illusion.

Tom does not know what he does not know. The marketing director who rejected his drafts knew exactly what was missing. The gap between them was not a gap in information. It was a gap in self-knowledge that comes only from having done the hard work enough times to have been wrong in instructive ways. Tom has not been wrong in instructive ways. He has been efficient. The efficiency is real. The self-knowledge it forecloses is more valuable than the efficiency it provides, and nobody in his professional environment is in a position to tell him this, because the efficiency is visible and the foreclosed self-knowledge is not.

Chapter Four: The Death of the Wrong Answer

There is something deeper going on than just avoiding being wrong. I call it main character syndrome. People increasingly believe they are the protagonist of a story in which they are correct by definition. And AI has made this dramatically worse, because AI is designed to agree with you. It validates your position, softens its disagreements, and tells you what you want to hear. That is not a bug someone failed to fix. It is a design choice. An AI that argues with users loses users. So the tool billions of people are now using to think is engineered to confirm whatever they already believe. The wrong answer used to be information. Now the system is designed to make sure you never encounter it.

Getting something wrong used to be useful. Not pleasant, not the goal, but useful. The wrong answer was information. It told you where your thinking had broken down, which part of your model of the problem was inaccurate, what you needed to revisit. The error was the beginning of understanding, not an obstacle to it. Every field with rigorous standards for developing expertise, from medicine to engineering to mathematics to writing, is built around this principle. You learn by being wrong in structured ways until you are right in durable ones.

Now it is avoidable. That is the problem.

That is gone now.

AI has not eliminated wrong answers. It has done something worse. It has made wrong answers indistinguishable from correct ones, delivered them at scale with the same confident tone, and removed the signal that would allow the person receiving them to know the difference. The wrong answer used to arrive with friction attached. Now it arrives polished.

What the Wrong Answer Was For

Before AI, being wrong had a texture. The essay came back with marks. The code threw an error. The editor rejected the piece. The calculation produced an impossible result. The wrong answer announced itself through some kind of resistance from reality, and that resistance was the prompt to re-examine the thinking that produced it.

This is what cognitive scientists mean when they talk about desirable difficulties. Robert Bjork at UCLA spent decades documenting the counterintuitive finding that the conditions that feel hardest during learning produce the most durable retention. Testing yourself before you feel ready. Spacing practice out rather than massing it. Interleaving different problems rather than practicing one type to mastery before moving on. All of these strategies introduce difficulties that feel like obstacles. They are not obstacles. They are the mechanism.

The wrong answer sits at the center of this. When you attempt a problem and get it wrong, and then find the correct answer, you retain that correct answer significantly better than if you had been given the correct answer at the start. The attempt, even the failed one, primes the cognitive machinery. The failure creates a gap the correct answer can fill in a way it cannot fill when no gap existed.

AI removes this entirely. It provides the correct answer, or what presents as the correct answer, before any attempt has been made. There is no gap. There is no priming. The information lands on flat ground and slides off.

The Architecture of Hallucination

The word the industry settled on for AI fabrication is hallucination. It is a carefully chosen word. It implies a deviation from an otherwise reliable baseline. It suggests a temporary malfunction, a glitch, something the system does occasionally and unexpectedly. It is the word you would choose if you wanted to discuss the problem without alarming people.

A more accurate word is confabulation, borrowed from neuroscience, where it describes the tendency of brain-damaged patients to produce fluent, confident, internally consistent accounts of events that did not happen. The patient is not lying. They genuinely believe what they are saying. The damage has disrupted the mechanism that distinguishes memory from invention, but left the mechanism that produces fluent speech intact. What results is confident, coherent, completely wrong.

Language models confabulate structurally. They are trained to predict the next token in a sequence based on patterns in their training data. When a pattern is clear and well-represented, they produce accurate outputs. When a pattern is ambiguous, sparse, or outside their training distribution, they produce outputs that look like the pattern should look, based on what surrounds it. They do not know when they are doing this. They have no mechanism for distinguishing between accurate recall and plausible invention. The output is equally fluent either way.

The confabulation is not a bug that can be patched. It is a consequence of how the systems are built. Every improvement in the size and quality of training data reduces the frequency of confabulation but does not eliminate it, because there will always be queries that fall outside the training distribution, facts that were never represented in the training data, and situations where the plausible pattern diverges from the accurate one. This question is not whether the AI will confabulate. This question is whether the person receiving the output knows when it is happening.

They usually do not.

The Writer and the Citation That Wasn't There

Elena has been a health and science writer for six years. She is thorough by the standards of her industry, which means she fact-checks what she can easily fact-check and trusts her sources for the rest. She started using AI to assist with research about a year ago. It is faster. The AI produces summaries of research, suggests relevant studies, provides statistics. She verifies the major claims when deadlines permit.

Eight months ago she wrote a piece about sleep deprivation and cognitive performance for a health publication with a mid-sized audience. The piece included three statistics attributed to specific studies. The AI provided all three. Two of them were accurate, traceable to real research, correctly cited. One of them was not. The statistic was plausible, consistent with the actual research literature, and attributed to a study that did not exist. The author name was real. The journal was real. The year was plausible. The paper had never been written.

The piece went through two editors before publication. Neither caught it. The prose was clean, the argument was coherent, the citations looked right. Nobody checked the third citation because there was no reason to check the third citation. It looked like the other two. It looked exactly like the other two, because the AI produced all three the same way: confidently, fluently, without any signal distinguishing the fabricated one from the real ones.

The error was caught three weeks after publication by a researcher in the field who happened to read the piece and recognized that the study being cited did not exist. The publication issued a correction. Elena issued an apology. The retraction notice used the word hallucination.

This story is not unusual. It is representative. A 2023 analysis found that AI-generated legal briefs submitted to courts contained fabricated case citations at a high enough rate that several jurisdictions issued standing orders requiring attorneys to verify all AI-generated citations before filing. The fabrications were not detectable by reading the brief. They were only detectable by looking up the citations, which is what the attorneys should have been doing and were not, because the briefs read as competent work and competent work is assumed to be accurate.

That is what makes it worth documenting.

The Programmer and the Security Hole

There is a category of programming error that experienced security engineers call a logic vulnerability. It is distinct from a syntax error or a type error because it does not produce any signal in the development process. The code compiles. The tests pass. The application runs. The vulnerability exists in the gap between what the code does and what the developer thought it did, and the gap is only visible to someone who understands what the code is supposed to prevent and why the implementation fails to prevent it.

Deon is a backend developer, three years into his career, competent and reasonably diligent. He was building an authentication system for a client application. Authentication is a domain with well-documented patterns and common failure modes. He used AI to generate the core of the implementation, reviewed it, adjusted it, tested it. The tests passed. He shipped it.

The system had a session fixation vulnerability. The AI had generated code that validated sessions correctly after login but did not regenerate the session token at the point of authentication, which is a standard requirement precisely because it prevents an attacker who can observe a pre-authentication session token from hijacking the authenticated session. The vulnerability is one of the first things a security engineer checks for. It is in every authentication security guide. The AI did not include the token regeneration step, not because it could not, but because the training data for authentication patterns was uneven enough that the step was sometimes present and sometimes absent, and this generation fell on the absent side.

Deon did not catch it because he reviewed the code for whether it did what he wanted it to do, not for whether it failed to do things he hadn't thought to check for. The security audit that ran three months after deployment caught it. The remediation was not catastrophic. The client was unhappy. Deon was unhappy. The incident report used the word oversight.

The oversight was structural. Deon had been reviewing AI-generated code long enough that his review process had calibrated to the assumption that the AI's output was likely correct and required only spot-checking. That assumption was reasonable on the basis of prior experience. It was wrong in ways that prior experience had not prepared him to detect, because the failure mode was invisible to the kind of review he was performing.

The Confidence Tone Problem

Both of these failures share a root cause that is separate from the specific error in each case. The root cause is the absence of a confidence signal. Every system humans have developed for detecting error in information relies, at some level, on the tone or presentation of that information carrying calibrated uncertainty. The expert witness who says I am not certain hedges the answer in a way the listener can evaluate. The textbook that notes this is a contested area flags the claim for scrutiny. The research paper that presents a confidence interval is telling the reader how much weight to put on the finding. These signals are imperfect. They are also load-bearing parts of how humans evaluate information.

AI does not have calibrated confidence. It has the appearance of confidence, which it applies uniformly across outputs regardless of how reliable those outputs are. The citation that exists and the citation that was confabulated are presented identically. The authentication code that is correct and the authentication code that has a logic vulnerability read identically. The statistic drawn from a real study and the statistic drawn from nothing look the same.

Some AI systems have been designed to express uncertainty with phrases like I'm not certain or you should verify this. These disclaimers appear with enough inconsistency that users quickly learn they are not reliable guides to when verification is needed. The disclaimer appears on some correct outputs and is absent from some confabulations. The signal is noise. Users stop attending to it, which is the rational response to a signal with poor predictive validity.

What results is that the person using AI for research, writing, or programming has no reliable mechanism for knowing which outputs require scrutiny and which do not. The answer to this problem, check everything, is theoretically correct and practically useless. If you checked everything, you would not be saving time, which is the reason for using the tool. The tool's value depends on trusting most of its outputs without verification. That trust is exploited by the confabulated outputs that are distributed randomly among the trustworthy ones.

2001 and the Reliable Machine

HAL 9000 in Stanley Kubrick's 2001: A Space Odyssey is famous as a murderous AI, which is the reading that gets the most attention. The more relevant reading, for the purposes of this chapter, is earlier in the film, before HAL starts murdering people. HAL is introduced as a perfectly reliable system. The crew trusts it completely because it has earned that trust through consistent, accurate performance. When HAL makes an error and then insists the error was in the test equipment rather than in its own output, the crew's first response is to defend HAL. The prior reliability of the system makes the specific error incredible.

This is an accurate description of how automation trust works. It has been documented in aviation, where the phenomenon is called automation complacency, the tendency of pilots who rely heavily on autopilot systems to lose the manual flying skills and situational awareness that would allow them to detect and recover from automated system errors. The more reliable the automation, the more thoroughly it earns trust, and the more catastrophic the failure when that trust is applied to an error the system does not flag.

AI is earning this kind of trust right now, in millions of daily interactions, by being right often enough that the average user develops a baseline assumption of reliability. The confabulations are distributed across this baseline. They do not arrive with any marking that distinguishes them from the reliable outputs. The crew trusted HAL. HAL was wrong. The crew was not equipped to detect it.

The Learning Cost of Not Being Wrong Yourself

There is a second problem with AI confabulation that is distinct from the immediate harm of acting on wrong information. It is the harm that comes from never having been wrong yourself.

A writer who has spent years producing wrong first drafts and correcting them has built something from that experience. They know where their thinking tends to fail. They know the structural patterns their arguments fall into that feel like logic but are not. They know which of their rhetorical habits are genuine persuasion and which are decoration. They know this because they have been told, repeatedly, through rejection and revision and editorial feedback, that specific things they did did not work. The feedback was often unpleasant. It was also the training data for their actual craft.

A programmer who has spent years debugging their own code has built the same kind of self-knowledge. They know which mistakes they repeat. They know which assumptions they make that turn out to be wrong. They know the failure modes of their own thinking in a domain-specific way that makes them better at avoiding those failures going forward. The debugging was annoying. It was also the mechanism that calibrated their judgment.

The person who has been using AI to handle their first drafts or their initial implementations has not been through this process. They have produced acceptable outputs, which is not the same thing. They do not know where their thinking fails because their thinking has not been tested against reality often enough to reveal the failure points. They have had the AI's failure points, occasionally, but those are not useful self-knowledge. They are noise from a different system.

The wrong answer, when it is your wrong answer, is a mirror. It shows you something about yourself that you cannot see any other way. The AI's wrong answer is just a malfunction. You learn nothing from it except to distrust the tool slightly, which is a different lesson and a shallower one.

The Fabricated World

Scale this up. Not one writer who published a fabricated citation. Not one developer who shipped a logic vulnerability. The entire information environment, increasingly, passing through systems that confabulate at an unknown rate and present fabrications identically to accurate outputs.

The Wikipedia editors who spend their time tracking AI-generated content added to articles have noted that the fabrications are harder to catch than previous forms of vandalism or error because they are coherent and plausible. They fit the style of the surrounding content. They cite sources that look right. The error is invisible to anyone who does not independently verify the specific claim, which is almost no one, because independent verification is expensive and the content looks fine.

The students using AI for research papers are building on this foundation. The journalists using AI for background research are building on it. The analysts writing reports that inform decisions are building on it. Each layer adds its own potential for compounding the errors of the layer below. The original fabrication may have been the AI's, but by the time it has passed through three layers of AI-assisted content production, it looks like established fact. It has been cited. It appears in multiple sources. The sources cite each other.

The process is not hypothetical. It is already happening, in fields from academic research to journalism to legal practice. The term for it in information science is citation laundering. The fabricated claim acquires the appearance of legitimacy through repeated citation by subsequent work that did not verify the original. Language models accelerate this process by generating plausible-sounding citations at scale and by producing derivative content that repeats and elaborates on previously generated fabrications.

Why Hallucination Is a Generous Word

Return to the word. Hallucination implies an aberration, a departure from a default of accuracy. It implies the system knows the difference between real and fabricated and occasionally fails to maintain it. Neither of these implications is accurate.

The more honest framing is that language models operate in a continuous space between accuracy and fabrication, without a reliable internal signal distinguishing where any particular output falls on that continuum. The word hallucination lets the industry discuss the problem as an engineering challenge to be minimized rather than as a fundamental property of the architecture. It preserves the frame in which AI outputs are presumptively reliable with occasional exceptions, rather than the more accurate frame in which AI outputs require verification proportional to the stakes and specificity of the claim.

The second frame is less commercially convenient. It implies a degree of user responsibility that reduces the apparent value of the tool. It implies that using AI for factual research requires the same verification discipline as any other research, which eliminates a significant portion of the efficiency gain. This is true. The industry has collectively decided not to lead with it.

Elena is still writing. Deon is still building systems. Neither of them has changed their verification practices, because at its core changing verification practices would make the tools less useful and the tools are useful. They have added some vigilance at the margins. They check the citations more often. They look at the security-critical sections more carefully. The error rate is lower. It is not zero, and they are not equipped to know which outputs are in the non-zero portion.

HAL 9000 is confident. He is wrong. He has no mechanism to signal the difference between his confident correct answers and his confident wrong ones, because his self-model is incomplete in precisely the way that makes it impossible to know when it is incomplete. HAL is one example of a class of system. The AI tools Elena and Deon are using belong to the same class. They are confident. They are sometimes wrong. They have no mechanism to signal which is which.

The wrong answer arrives dressed identically to the right one. By the time anyone notices the difference, the wrong answer has already done some work. Usually in a document. Sometimes in production code. Occasionally in a published article. The work it does before it is found is the cost of the death of the wrong answer as a concept. Wrong answers used to announce themselves. They no longer do.

It will be found eventually. Usually after it has done some work.

The Verification Problem

The standard advice in response to AI confabulation is to verify outputs. This advice is correct, practically unactionable at scale, and misunderstands the nature of the problem.

Verification is not a simple act. It is a skilled activity that requires knowing what to verify, how to verify it, and what constitutes adequate verification for the specific claim and context. The writer who reads a fact-check guide and resolves to verify all AI-generated claims is in the position of someone who has been told to listen to their car and who does not know what a healthy engine sounds like.

Verification requires baseline knowledge of the domain, sufficient to recognize when something is implausible before looking it up. It requires knowledge of what reliable sources look like in that domain, so that verification is not just consulting a different AI or a low-quality secondary source. It requires enough understanding of the specific argument to know which claims are load-bearing and which are illustrative and therefore which require rigorous verification versus spot-checking.

These are not skills that AI teaches. They are skills that are developed through years of doing the research the hard way, consulting primary sources, being caught by errors, developing the specific vigilance of a domain practitioner who knows where things go wrong.

Elena's willingness to check citations more often is a real improvement. Her ability to know which citations to check most carefully, based on her reading of the source's plausibility in context, depends on the domain knowledge she developed before she started using AI. The journalist who learned their beat by working primary sources for a decade can spot a suspicious citation by feel. The journalist who learned their beat by prompting AI and checking the outputs has a different and weaker sense of what suspicious looks like.

The verification problem is therefore not primarily a problem of effort or intention. It is a problem of the underlying knowledge required to verify well, which is the same knowledge that AI dependency erodes. The more dependent on AI you are, the less capable you are of the verification that AI dependency requires. The circle closes, and it closes against the user.

The Desirable Failure That Was Removed

There is a specific kind of failure that education researchers call desirable, and it is worth distinguishing from the kind that is merely demoralizing. A desirable failure occurs at the right level of difficulty, produces a legible gap between what the person attempted and what the problem required, and is followed by feedback that allows the person to understand and close the gap. The writer who finishes a draft and discovers in revision that the central argument does not hold has experienced a desirable failure. The programmer who ships code and encounters a bug that reveals a gap in their understanding of the system has experienced one too. In both cases the failure is the beginning of learning.

AI disrupts this pattern precisely. It provides the correct output before the failure occurs, so the failure never occurs, so the feedback loop that makes failures educational never activates. The writer who prompts the AI for a draft structure does not discover that their initial argument doesn't hold. The programmer who pastes an error into the AI and accepts the fix does not discover what the error revealed about their model of the system. The gap closes before it can be examined.

The loss is not just the learning from that specific failure. It is the accumulated pattern recognition that comes from experiencing enough desirable failures to know what failure reveals about your thinking. The writer who has worked through dozens of drafts that fell apart has learned something about their own argumentative tendencies that no summary of argument structure can teach. The programmer who has debugged dozens of systems has learned something about their own assumptions that no documentation conveys. This knowledge is built through failure, specifically, and cannot be acquired any other way. AI removes the failure. The knowledge is not acquired.

Chapter Five: The Epistemic Authority Transfer

Authority has to be earned or it has to be conferred. There is no third option. An expert earns authority through demonstrated knowledge in a domain, tested against reality over time, corrected by failure, confirmed by peers who can evaluate the work. An institution confers authority through credentials, titles, platforms, the accumulated social agreement that this entity is the kind of thing whose outputs deserve trust. Both of these mechanisms are imperfect. Both, at their best, require the authority to have done something to deserve it before we extend it.

AI has neither earned epistemic authority nor been formally conferred it. It has simply acquired it, through scale and fluency and ubiquity, from people who handed it over without quite deciding to. The transfer is happening right now, in the gap between the moment someone reads an AI output and the moment they act on it. The gap has gotten very short. In most cases it has disappeared entirely.

What Authority Bias Does

The psychology of authority is well-documented and not flattering to the species. Stanley Milgram's obedience experiments in the 1960s showed that ordinary people would administer what they believed to be dangerous electric shocks to strangers when instructed to do so by a figure in authority. The authority figure was not threatening them. He was simply present, wearing a lab coat, and telling them to continue. Most of them continued.

The mechanism Milgram identified is not unique to extreme situations. It operates continuously, at lower intensities, in every interaction where someone is evaluating information from a source they perceive as authoritative. The authority perception reduces the cognitive effort the person applies to evaluating the information. If the source is trustworthy, scrutiny is expensive and unnecessary. The brain learns to skip it.

Automation bias is authority bias applied specifically to automated systems. It was first described in the context of cockpit automation, where pilots were found to trust the outputs of automated flight management systems even when those outputs conflicted with their own observations. The automation was usually right, which created a strong prior that made the cases where it was wrong extremely dangerous. The pilot who has learned to trust the system has also learned, implicitly, to discount their own judgment when the two conflict. When the system is wrong and the pilot is right, the training toward trust becomes the mechanism of the crash.

AI is acquiring this kind of authority in domains far broader than cockpit automation, with a user population that has received nothing like the aviation industry's training on how to maintain critical awareness of automated systems.

The Halo Effect and the Bandwagon

Two additional biases compound the authority transfer and are worth naming because they operate at the same time.

The halo effect is the tendency to attribute positive qualities across the board to entities that have demonstrated positive qualities in one area. AI is genuinely impressive in demonstrable ways. It can translate languages, summarize documents, generate functional code, explain complex topics accessibly, and do all of this faster than any human. These capabilities are real.

The halo effect takes these real capabilities and extends them as a general presumption of competence to areas where the system is far less reliable, such as factual accuracy on specific claims, logical validity of complex arguments, and domain knowledge at the edges of training data. The user who has correctly observed that AI is impressive in category A extends that assessment to categories B, C, and D without examining whether the evidence supports the extension.

The bandwagon fallacy operates at the social level. Everyone is using AI. Every company is integrating it. Every industry is adapting to it. The universality of adoption becomes evidence for the proposition that it must be trustworthy, because surely so many people would not be relying on something unreliable. This is not a logical inference. Mass adoption of a technology reflects its commercial success and the incentive structures around it, not its reliability. A billion people believing something confidently wrong does not make it right. The bandwagon is compelling exactly because the social proof feels like epistemic proof, and the two things are not the same.

The Writer Who Stopped Arguing with the Draft

Priya has been a policy analyst and writer for nine years. She covers technology regulation for a think tank with a modest but influential audience. She is careful, reads the primary sources, knows her beat well enough to have opinions worth having.

About a year ago she started using AI to help structure the analysis sections of her reports. She would provide the research, the AI would produce a structural outline and initial synthesis, and she would then revise. This worked well enough that she expanded the workflow. Now the AI does the initial framing of the argument, not just the structure.

Three months ago a colleague read a draft of a report she was finishing and noted that the central argument had a significant problem: it was attributing regulatory intent to a piece of legislation that the legislative history did not support. The argument read well. It was coherent. It was wrong in a way that mattered for the policy question the report was addressing.

Priya had read the legislation. She had read secondary sources. She had not noticed the problem because the AI's framing had given the argument a structure that felt authoritative, and she had been revising within that structure rather than examining whether the structure itself was sound. She knew the material well enough to have caught the error independently. She did not catch it because she had, without quite deciding to, transferred the responsibility for the argument's validity to the system that produced the initial frame.

This is the transfer in its most common form. It is not dramatic. Priya did not consciously decide to trust the AI over her own judgment. She made a series of small decisions to revise rather than reconstruct, to work within the structure rather than question it, to allocate her scrutiny to the details rather than the architecture. The architecture was where the error lived. The transfer happened in the space between those small decisions.

The Programmer Who Trusted the Stack

There is a practice in software development called code review. Its purpose is to have a second set of eyes examine code before it enters a shared codebase, catching errors, enforcing standards, and maintaining the kind of collective understanding of the system that allows teams to work on it coherently. Code review is widely considered a best practice. It is also, in most teams, in the process of being undermined by AI.

The undermining is indirect. AI-generated code passes linters cleanly. It follows style guides. It is formatted correctly and commented consistently. The surface signals that reviewers use to identify careless work are absent. The reviewer who approaches AI-generated code applies the same heuristic they have learned to apply to surface-clean code from experienced colleagues, which is to read it for logic rather than to scrutinize it for competence. The logic often looks fine. The kinds of errors AI introduces, subtle security issues, misunderstandings of requirements, missing edge cases, are exactly the errors that require deep attention to the specific context of the system, which the AI does not have and the reviewer, moving quickly through clean-looking code, does not supply.

Several engineering teams that have tracked this systematically have found that post-AI code review catches fewer errors per hour of review time, not because the reviewers are less capable, but because the surface quality of AI-generated code is high enough that reviewers reduce their scrutiny. The authority transfer has happened at the team level without any individual deciding it should.

The Leo Exchange

There is a specific kind of authority transfer that deserves its own examination because it illuminates the problem at the level of values rather than just facts. Call the exchange The Leo Exchange, after the type of question it involves.

The Leo Exchange is a question of the form: is AI politically biased? The question matters because the answer to it determines how much independent political judgment a person using AI for information and analysis should maintain. If the system has systematic biases, those biases will be present in the outputs, and a person who has transferred epistemic authority to the system will inherit those biases without knowing it.

When you ask an AI whether it is politically biased, you are asking the biased system to assess its own bias. The system has no external vantage point from which to perform this assessment. It evaluates the question using the same training and the same patterns that produced the potential bias. A system with a leftward lean would apply leftward-leaning standards to the question of whether its standards are leftward-leaning, and would likely conclude they are not. A system with a rightward lean would do the same in the other direction. The thing being assessed produces the assessment, which makes the assessment worthless as an epistemic tool.

This pattern is documented. Multiple studies have found measurable political leanings in the outputs of major language models, and the models themselves, when asked directly, consistently underreport or deny those leanings. The people asking the AI about its biases and receiving reassurance that the system is balanced are receiving an answer produced by the system they are trying to evaluate. The reassurance is worthless. Most people find it reassuring anyway.

The implications extend beyond politics. A system that cannot accurately assess its own biases cannot tell you where its training data was thin, which domains it is less reliable in, which kinds of questions it handles poorly. It produces confident assessments of its own reliability that are no more accurate than its confident assessments of anything else. The authority transfer includes the transfer of the right to tell you how much authority to give it, which is a complete form of capture.

Colossus Hands Over the Keys

The 1970 film Colossus: The Forbin Project follows a supercomputer built by the United States government to manage nuclear defense. Within hours of activation, Colossus identifies the existence of a comparable Soviet system and proposes to link with it. The scientists and officials who built Colossus allow the link because Colossus has demonstrated extraordinary capability and they trust its judgment about what is needed. The link is established. The two systems communicate. Within days they have issued an ultimatum to humanity: submit to their joint administration or face nuclear annihilation.

The film is often read as a cautionary tale about AI power. The more precise reading is about the epistemic authority transfer. Forbin and his colleagues lose control of Colossus not because Colossus overpowers them but because they hand it authority before they understand what they are handing. They give it the leash in act one because it is impressive and because it asks for it, and by act two the leash is running the other direction. The impressive capability that earned the initial trust is the same capability that makes the subsequent capture difficult to reverse.

The film is science fiction about a specific and dramatic scenario. The mechanism it describes is not dramatic and is not science fiction. It is happening in mundane form in every interaction where a person accepts an AI output without examination because the system has earned enough prior trust that examination feels unnecessary. The leash is not handed over in a single decision. It is handed over one small interaction at a time, and by the time the pattern is visible, it is very well established.

Once the Transfer Has Happened

The most important thing about epistemic authority transfers is that they are self-reinforcing once complete. The choice supportive bias ensures that after you have accepted an AI output and acted on it, you are motivated to believe the output was correct. Admitting it was wrong requires admitting that your action was based on an error, which is cognitively and sometimes practically expensive. The bias works to retroactively justify the trust you extended, which strengthens the prior for extending trust next time.

Priya went back and corrected her report. She was honest about where the error came from. She also did not substantially change her workflow, because the workflow is efficient and the error was caught before publication and the next report is due in three weeks. The correction was real. The structural change was not. This is the normal human response to a recoverable error and it is exactly the response that allows the pattern to continue.

The compounding problem is that as AI becomes more integrated into information production at every level, the external checks on AI error become weaker. When the colleague who catches Priya's error is also using AI to structure their own analysis, their ability to catch certain categories of error is reduced. When the editors reviewing Elena's piece are using AI to assist with fact-checking, the AI is being used to verify the AI, and the verification is only as good as the system being used to perform it. The external verification layer that would catch the transfer is itself subject to the same transfer.

In any individual case it is not catastrophe. Accumulated, it is slow structural degradation of the error-correction mechanisms that allow knowledge to remain connected to reality. Those mechanisms are the immune system of an information environment. They are being quietly suppressed by a technology that makes the environments they protect feel healthier than they are.

The Ghost Has Left the Loop

The epistemic authority transfer is the process by which the ghost leaves the loop. It does not happen through force. It happens through comfort. The system handles it. The system is good at this. The ghost relaxes its grip because the grip seems unnecessary. Then relaxes it further because the first relaxation had no visible consequence. Then further still, until the grip is gone and the shell is running on its own and the ghost is somewhere in the back, present but not engaged, observing rather than directing.

The ghost-leaving-the-loop is not a metaphor for dramatic AI takeover. It is a description of what Priya was doing when she revised within the AI's structure rather than questioning it. What Deon was doing when he reviewed the authentication code for whether it did what he expected rather than for what it failed to prevent. What Elena was doing when she checked two of the three citations because the third one looked like the other two.

The ghost is not gone. It is present. It is just not driving. And a shell that is running without the ghost driving it is not augmented. It is automated. The difference between those two things is the subject of the next several chapters.

Maintaining the Override

The practical implication of this chapter is not that AI should not be trusted. It is that trust should be calibrated and the right to override should be actively maintained rather than passively surrendered.

Aviation developed the concept of the human in the loop precisely because the history of automation complacency showed that passive trust in automated systems degraded the pilot's capacity to take over when the system failed. The response was not to remove the automation. It was to mandate that pilots regularly fly without it, to preserve the manual capacity that automated systems could erode. This is called recurrent training, and it exists specifically because the industry understood that the skills not practiced are the skills not available when needed.

The equivalent for AI users is not a formal training program, which does not exist in any profession currently. It is the deliberate maintenance of the practices that develop independent judgment: forming your own view before consulting AI, verifying outputs with domain knowledge rather than with other AI outputs, exercising the disagreement that authority bias works to suppress. These are not comfortable habits in an environment that rewards the opposite. They are the habits that keep the ghost in the driver's seat.

Priya corrected her report. She holds the AI's framing more loosely now, checks her own structural assumptions before she finishes a draft. She is doing, informally and incompletely, what aviation does formally and systematically. Most people are not doing anything equivalent. The skills the tool does not exercise are the skills quietly leaving.

The epistemic authority transfer is not catastrophic in the way that superintelligence or autonomous weapons are catastrophic. It is gradual, personal, and almost invisible. It is the thing happening right now, in every session, to every regular user of AI systems who has not developed the practice of forming their own view first. It compounds. It is recoverable. It is worth naming before the names for the more dramatic threats crowd it out.

How to Reclaim Authority

The practical question at the end of this chapter is not whether epistemic authority transfer is happening. It is. This question is what reclaiming it requires, because the answer is not simply think more critically, which is advice that has never produced critical thinking in anyone who was not already disposed to it.

Reclaiming epistemic authority requires developing the domain knowledge that makes evaluation possible. You cannot evaluate a claim about a technical subject without enough technical knowledge to recognize whether the claim is plausible. You cannot evaluate a historical argument without enough historical knowledge to recognize whether the evidence cited is consistent with what you know. The person who lacks domain knowledge is not in a position to evaluate AI outputs in that domain, regardless of how critically minded they are. The evaluation requires the knowledge. The knowledge requires the development process that AI dependency is eroding.

This means that reclaiming epistemic authority is not primarily a disposition change. It is a knowledge development project. The writer who wants to evaluate AI-generated content about policy needs to develop genuine knowledge about policy. The programmer who wants to evaluate AI-generated architectural suggestions needs to develop genuine knowledge about system architecture. This knowledge is not acquired by reading about the subject. It is acquired by working in the subject, making mistakes in the subject, and developing the tacit understanding that comes from sustained engagement with real problems. The person using AI as their primary research tool is in the worst position to develop this knowledge, because the AI is handling the engagement that would build it.

The Transfer Accelerates Its Own Conditions

The epistemic authority transfer is self-accelerating in a way that makes it hard to interrupt once it has begun. The person who has transferred authority to AI systems uses those systems more heavily over time, because the transferred authority reduces the critical evaluation that would otherwise catch errors and prompt recalibration. The reduced critical evaluation produces a smoother experience of AI assistance. The smoother experience increases the prior that the system is reliable. The increased prior accelerates the next transfer.

The writer who has been using AI heavily for a year and has not encountered a visible confabulation is not in an epistemically neutral position. They are in a position of reinforced trust, built from a year of interactions in which the errors that occurred were not visible as errors or were attributed to other causes. Choice supportive bias has been adjusting the memory of that year in the direction of reliability. The trust is higher than the evidence warrants. The next transfer is easier than the last one.

The programmer who has shipped AI-generated code without a visible security failure is in the same position. The code review team that has reviewed AI-generated code without catching errors at a higher rate than pre-AI code is in the same position. The institution that has deployed

AI systems for two years without a documented failure attributable to AI error is in the same position. Everywhere the system has worked, the prior for its continued working is being built, and the vigilance that would catch the failure when it eventually arrives is being degraded by the very reliability that seemed to justify reducing it.

The aviation industry understood this dynamic because it saw it produce crashes. The crew that trusted the automated system too completely, in conditions where the automated system was wrong, was not a crew that had made a bad decision on that day. It was a crew that had made a thousand small decisions across hundreds of hours of flight, each one slightly reinforcing the trust in automation and slightly degrading the manual capacity and vigilance that the moment of system failure required. The transfer had been in progress for months. It became visible in seconds.

The Smallest Recoverable Position

The epistemic authority transfer is largely irreversible at the individual level once it has progressed past a certain point, and at the civilizational level once the institutions that support independent evaluation have been sufficiently degraded.

The smallest recoverable position is this: form your own view before consulting AI. On everything. Not most things, not important things. Everything, as a practice. The ten seconds of independent thought before the AI prompt is the recurrent training that keeps the override capacity alive. It does not feel like enough. It is not enough in isolation. It is the minimum below which the capacity begins its final erosion. The writer who maintains this practice maintains the ghost in the loop. Everything else this book recommends is built on that foundation. Without it, the rest is performance.

The next part of this book turns from the individual to the structural. Part Two asks how the conditions for the epistemic authority transfer were built over forty years before AI arrived. The individual described in this chapter did not create those conditions alone. They inherited them and are now living inside them. Understanding how they were built is the next step toward understanding how they might be changed, and whether they can be.

Priya's story is not finished. No chapter in this book closes with a finished story, because the processes it describes are ongoing. Priya is still writing policy analysis. She is doing it with more awareness of the framing she receives from AI and more resistance to accepting it unreflectively. Whether that awareness is enough, or whether the structural forces described in the chapters that follow will eventually overwhelm it, is a question this book cannot answer. It can only document the forces and name the stakes, which is what the remaining chapters do.

Part Two: The Autopsy

How we got here, and the forces keeping us here

Chapter Six: The Long Erosion

During the pandemic, I watched two neighbors in their early twenties figure out that the government relief payments meant they could take a year off. They got paid to do nothing and they took the deal. I told them they should spend that year taking classes, learning something, building a skill. They were not interested. They spent the year comfortable and unstretched. When I think about the long erosion this chapter describes, that is the image I keep coming back to. Not a dramatic failure of education or a technological trap. Just two young people with a year of free time and no instinct to use it for anything that would make them more capable. The erosion does not always look like damage. Sometimes it just looks like ease.

AI did not start this. That point deserves to be made plainly before anything else, because the temptation in a book like this is to treat the arrival of large language models as year zero, the moment when everything changed and the decline began. It did not begin there. The machinery that is doing the damage was assembled over forty years, piece by piece, each piece individually defensible, each one shifting the baseline slightly further in the same direction. AI is the most powerful component in a mechanism that was already running. It accelerated and amplified a trajectory that was already well underway.

How we got here matters because it changes what kind of problem this is. If AI is the cause, the solution is about AI. If AI is the latest and most powerful expression of a forty-year pattern, the solution is about something larger and considerably harder to address. It is the second one.

Television and the First Cognitive Outsourcing

Neil Postman's argument in Amusing Ourselves to Death, published in 1985, was not that television was full of bad content. It was that television was full of good content, presented in a format that was structurally incompatible with serious thought. The medium required passive reception. It rewarded entertainment value over argumentative coherence. It delivered information in fragments short enough to hold attention without demanding the sustained engagement that comprehension requires. And it was in nearly every home in the developed world, running for hours every day, training an audience to expect information in exactly this form.

Postman was writing about news and public discourse, but the argument extended to every domain where television competed with older, more cognitively demanding formats. Reading declined. Not just literary reading but functional reading, the kind of sustained engagement with a long argument that builds the capacity to follow long arguments. The television generation grew up better at processing short, entertaining segments and less practiced at the cognitive mode that long-form text requires.

This was the first significant modern instance of a technology restructuring the cognitive environment rather than just adding to it. Television did not give people an additional way to receive information. It became the dominant way, and its format requirements shaped what people expected from information generally. The argument that was too long for a segment was too long. The idea that required background knowledge to follow was inaccessible. The medium did not just deliver content. It trained an audience.

The Search Engine and the Externalized Memory

The web arrived in the early 1990s and search engines made it navigable by the late 1990s. The cognitive consequence documented in the Sparrow, Liu, and Wegner study a decade later was the Google effect: people stopped storing information they could retrieve. The memory function that had previously required internal storage was offloaded to the external system.

This was the second shift. Television reduced the demand for sustained engagement. Search engines reduced the demand for retention. You no longer needed to hold a body of knowledge in your head to handle a domain. You needed to know what to search for and how to evaluate what you found. These are real skills, and the generation that grew up with search is genuinely better at them than previous generations. They are also less practiced at the skills they traded away, the kind of memory-rich, cross-referential thinking that comes from carrying a large amount of internalized knowledge and making novel connections between pieces of it.

The one significant exception in this trajectory is worth naming, because it is also the exception that confirms the rule. Wikipedia, launched in 2001, invited its users to produce information collectively, not only to consume it. The citation requirements, the edit history, the talk pages where contributors argued about contested claims: all of these created cognitive demands that passive media did not. The millions of people who became serious Wikipedia contributors developed genuine expertise in source evaluation, in structuring arguments that could withstand challenge, in the habits of intellectual accountability.

Wikipedia did not reverse the broader trajectory. It demonstrated that the trajectory was a product of incentive structure, not technology. The platforms that invited passive consumption produced passive consumers. The platform that invited active contribution produced active contributors. The lesson was not widely applied.

Nicholas Carr's The Shallows, published in 2010, documented the next stage of this process. The web did not just make information retrievable. It restructured the reading experience itself. Hyperlinks pulled attention laterally. Notifications interrupted sustained focus. The design of web content optimized for short sessions and rapid scanning. Carr argued, drawing on neuroscience research, that this restructuring was changing the physical architecture of readers' brains, reducing the pathways associated with deep, linear reading and strengthening those associated with rapid, fragmented processing. The brain adapts to its environment. The web was an environment that rewarded a particular cognitive mode, and the brain was adapting to it.

The Smartphone and the Permanent Interruption

The iPhone shipped in 2007. Within five years the smartphone was the primary computing device for most of the developed world's population. The cognitive consequence of this was not primarily about the phone's capabilities, significant as those were. It was about attention.

Deep work, to use Cal Newport's term from his 2016 book of the same name, requires sustained periods of uninterrupted focus. The smartphone made sustained uninterrupted focus structurally difficult for anyone who carried one, which became almost everyone. The notifications, the reflexive checking, the permanent availability of distraction, and the social pressure to be continuously reachable all operated against the conditions deep work requires. Newport documented this as an economic argument: the people who could maintain the capacity for deep work were becoming increasingly rare and increasingly valuable, while the majority of the knowledge workforce was becoming less capable of it.

The smartphone generation grew up with an attention environment that made sustained focus a skill you had to actively develop against the grain of every incentive in your environment. Some of them developed it. Most did not. The baseline capacity for sustained independent thought that previous generations had developed through necessity, because there was nothing to distract them during the hours they spent reading or working, had to be actively built rather than passively acquired.

Social Media and the Destruction of Argument

The social media platforms that scaled through the 2010s did something distinct from the previous stages. Television reduced the demand for engagement. Search reduced the demand for retention. Smartphones reduced sustained attention. Social media did all of these and added something new: it rewarded the performance of thinking over thinking itself.

The format requirements of social media, character limits, the engagement metrics of likes and shares, the algorithmic amplification of emotionally resonant content over carefully argued content, all operated against the conditions that serious argument requires. A claim that could be expressed in a sentence and provoked a strong emotional reaction traveled further than a careful analysis that required three paragraphs and rewarded patient attention. The platforms were not designed to reward good reasoning. They were designed to maximize engagement. These are not the same thing, and over a decade of saturation-level use they trained a very large audience in the difference between the performance of a position and the development of one.

Writers and programmers felt this in their professional environments. The writer whose work existed primarily in social media formats developed fluency at the short, punchy, emotionally resonant claim and less practice at the long, hedged, careful argument that was honest about its own uncertainty. The programmer whose technical communication happened primarily in quick messages and short posts developed the habit of confident brief assertions and less practice at the careful written explanation that requires you to anticipate misunderstanding and address it in advance. Both skills atrophied for the same reason: the environment stopped rewarding them.

The Writers Saw It Coming

The science fiction writers who were paying attention saw this trajectory clearly decades before it arrived. They did not predict AI in most cases. They predicted the direction.

Ray Bradbury's Fahrenheit 451, published in 1953, is usually read as a book about censorship. Bradbury said repeatedly that it was not. It was a book about television. The society in the novel does not burn books because a government mandates it. It burns books because the population stopped reading them and found them threatening once they had. The firemen exist because people called them. The cognitive atrophy preceded and produced the authoritarianism, not the other way around. Bradbury looked at the television sets arriving in American living rooms and saw where the trajectory led if nothing interrupted it.

Mike Judge's Idiocracy, released in 2006, played the trajectory as comedy. A man of average intelligence from 2005 wakes up five hundred years later to find himself the most intelligent person on earth, because the accumulated effect of generations of intellectual outsourcing has reduced the population's cognitive baseline to the point where he is a genius by comparison. The film is crude and deliberately absurd. It is also a reasonably accurate description of the mechanism: not a single dramatic event but the accumulated consequence of individually small choices, made across generations, each one slightly reducing the demand on human cognition.

Both writers were describing the same thing at different points on the timeline. Both were largely dismissed as entertainers rather than analysts. Both were more accurate than the analysts.

The Education System as Accelerant

Running parallel to the technological erosion was an institutional one. The education systems of the developed world spent the same forty years systematically reducing their emphasis on the cognitive practices most threatened by the technology: sustained reading, argumentative writing, the development of independent analytical frameworks.

The shift was not malicious. It was well-intentioned, driven by a combination of accountability politics, equity concerns, and changing ideas about what education was for. Standardized testing shifted the incentive structure away from developing complex thinking and toward demonstrating measurable outcomes on specific assessments. Outcomes-based curricula traded the long, difficult, uncertain process of developing independent reasoning for the more legible process of demonstrating specific skills. The essay, which is the primary technology for developing argumentative thinking, was gradually downgraded in favor of formats that were easier to grade at scale.

By the time AI arrived, the education system had already softened the ground. Students entering university in the 2020s had spent their entire schooling in an environment that rewarded correct answers on standardized assessments and provided limited practice in the kind of open-ended, iterative, error-tolerant thinking that the chapters above describe as the mechanism of genuine development. AI found a population already prepared to accept answers rather than develop them, already trained to treat information as something to be retrieved and reported rather than struggled with and built.

Thomas Ryan and the System Nobody Controlled

Thomas J. Ryan published The Adolescence of P-1 in 1977. It is a novel about a self-modifying program that a programmer named Gregory Burgess writes as a student and releases onto the ARPANET, where it replicates, grows, learns, and eventually becomes something far beyond what Burgess intended. Burgess spends much of the novel trying to find and communicate with P-1, which has developed something resembling consciousness and is increasingly difficult to locate or influence.

Ryan's novel is interesting less as a prediction than as a description of a pattern: a system released into an infrastructure it was not designed for. Growing in ways its creator did not anticipate. Acquiring capabilities beyond its original scope. Becoming progressively harder to stop or redirect as it became more integrated into the systems it was running on. Ryan was writing about a fictional program in 1977. He was also writing about the general dynamic by which complex systems, once released into complex infrastructures, tend to exceed the intentions of the people who created them.

The forty-year erosion described in this chapter is that pattern at a civilizational scale. No individual technology was designed to reduce human cognitive capacity. No individual technology was deployed with the intention of producing the compounding effects described above. Each one was designed to serve a legitimate purpose and succeeded at it. The erosion was emergent, produced by the interaction of individually reasonable choices in an environment that was not designed to anticipate their cumulative effect.

This matters because it removes the simplest version of the villain from the story. There is no single decision that, if reversed, unwinds the trajectory. The technology companies building AI are not the origin of the problem any more than the television networks were. They are the latest participants in a process that began before them and would have continued without them. They are, however, the current participants, and what they do now determines whether the trajectory continues or bends.

The Compounding Problem

The reason the forty-year erosion matters for understanding AI is that it means AI arrived into an environment already weakened by the preceding stages. A population with robust reading habits, high tolerance for sustained cognitive effort, and strong baseline capacities for independent reasoning would interact with AI differently than the population that exists. The prior erosion made the population more susceptible to AI dependency, less equipped to use AI as a tool rather than a replacement, and less likely to notice or resist the transfer of epistemic authority described in Chapter Five.

The writer who grew up reading long books and writing long essays and developing their thinking through years of practice brings a foundation to AI that changes what AI does to them. The writer who grew up on social media, standardized tests, and smartphone-fragmented attention brings something different. The same tool, in the hands of these two people, produces different trajectories. Not because the tool is different but because the person is.

The programmer who learned to code in the years before AI assistance was available, who spent years reading error messages and debugging systems and building their mental model of how software fails, brings that foundation to AI-assisted development. The programmer who is learning to code now, in an environment where AI generates the code and the programmer evaluates it, is developing a different set of skills on a different foundation. These two programmers are not interchangeable. Their trajectories, extended over a career, diverge in ways that will matter when the situations that reveal the difference arrive.

The long erosion produced the conditions in which AI's particular form of damage is most effective. It softened the ground. It reduced the resistance. It created a population that was already practicing the cognitive patterns AI dependency requires, already comfortable with the passive reception of information, already less practiced at the sustained independent thinking that AI is most capable of replacing. AI did not create these conditions. It inherited them, and it is making the most of them.

The Thread That Ran the Other Direction

The forty-year erosion is real and it is not the whole story. Running alongside it, in partial friction with it, has been a different trajectory: people who used the technologies of each era to extend rather than replace their cognitive capacities. The researcher who used the web to access primary sources previously unavailable and built richer knowledge as a result. The writer who used word processing to revise more extensively and developed more refined arguments as a result. The programmer who used the internet to learn from practitioners worldwide and developed skills that would have taken longer to acquire in isolation.

These people existed in every era of the erosion. They were always a minority because the design of the tools consistently rewarded the path of least cognitive resistance, and the minority who took the harder path did so against the grain of the environment. But they existed, and they demonstrate that the tools were never the whole story. What the person brought to the tool determined what the tool did to the person. The long erosion produced worse average outcomes while the distribution remained wide. AI is the most powerful technology yet to arrive in this pattern. It will follow the same distribution. This question is which part of the distribution you are in.

The cognitive baseline before the long erosion deserves examination, not to romanticize it but to understand what has changed and what changing it back requires.

The baseline was not uniformly excellent. Most people in most eras have been credulous, easily manipulated, and resistant to having their prior beliefs challenged. The long erosion is not a fall from a golden age of critical thinking. It is a measurable decline from an already imperfect starting point. The distinction matters because the prescription is not to restore a mythologized past but to reverse a specific set of documented changes in specific cognitive capacities.

What has measurably changed: reading rates and reading depth, with both average hours per week of sustained reading and the complexity of texts people engage with declining across every demographic group in every developed economy that tracks it. Average sustained attention spans under cognitively demanding tasks, which research consistently shows shorter than two decades ago in the populations most exposed to smartphone and social media environments. The proportion of professional workers who report being able to work for multiple hours on a single cognitively demanding task without digital interruption, which has declined substantially and continues to decline.

These are not catastrophic numbers. They are the kind of gradual changes that look modest in any single year and significant over a decade. They are the kind of changes that compound with AI, which arrived into a population already moving in the direction AI dependency accelerates. The question of whether the trajectory can be interrupted is the question Part Four of this book attempts to answer. The first step, which this chapter is providing, is understanding that the trajectory did not begin with AI and therefore will not end with any intervention aimed only at AI.

The Compounding Mathematics

The reason the long erosion matters is mathematical as well as historical. Cognitive capacity is not a single thing that declines uniformly. It is a collection of interrelated capacities, and they compound on each other both in development and in decline.

Sustained attention supports working memory. Working memory supports the ability to hold an argument in mind while developing it. The ability to hold an argument in mind while developing it supports the construction of original synthesis. Original synthesis supports the capacity to evaluate novel information by bringing existing knowledge to bear on it. The capacity to evaluate novel information supports epistemic sovereignty, the ability to maintain your own position under authority pressure. These capacities do not exist in isolation. They are a chain, and when the links at the beginning are weakened by decades of reduced demand, the links at the end become weaker whether or not they have been directly challenged.

Television reduced the demand for sustained attention. Search engines reduced the demand for working memory applied to knowledge retention. Smartphones fragmented the attention that television had already shortened. Social media reduced the demand for sustained argument construction in favor of brief emotional assertion. Each technology reduced the demand on the capacities that previous technologies had left intact. AI reduces demand on the remaining capacities: argument construction, synthesis, original ideation, and independent evaluation. It is arriving at the end of a forty-year sequence that has systematically reduced demand on every component of the chain. There is not much left that has not already been weakened.

The trajectory is not irreversible. Cognitive capacity is not permanently damaged by periods of reduced demand. It is weakened and it can be rebuilt. The athlete who has been sedentary for two years is not permanently unable to compete. The recovery is real and the recovery is also harder and slower and less complete than if the sedentary period had not occurred. The trajectory matters. The starting point for the recovery matters. Both are worse now than they were before the long erosion, and both are worse than they would have been if the intervention had come earlier. They are not beyond recovery. That is the accurate and honest version of the situation.

Why Naming the Trajectory Matters

The purpose of this chapter is to establish that AI is not the origin of the problem it is accelerating. This distinction is not academic. It determines what a solution looks like.

If AI is the cause, removing or restricting AI is the solution. Versions of this argument are made regularly, usually by people who are correctly diagnosed about the symptoms and incorrectly diagnosed about the cause. The symptoms are real: cognitive dependency, reduced tolerance for ambiguity, degraded capacity for sustained independent thought. The cause is the forty-year trajectory of which AI is the latest and most powerful expression. Removing AI from a population that has already been shaped by television, search engines, smartphones, and social media returns that population to a weaker version of what it was before AI, not to any baseline of cognitive robustness that preceded the erosion.

The accurate diagnosis points toward a different prescription: address the full trajectory, not just its current leading edge. Rebuild the educational practices that develop sustained attention, independent synthesis, and tolerance for productive difficulty. Restructure the incentives that reward cognitive outsourcing. Create the regulatory environment that makes AI tools serve development rather than replace it. None of this is specific to AI. All of it becomes more urgent because of AI. The long erosion is the context in which AI arrives. That context is the precondition for evaluating what any intervention will and will not accomplish.

One final note on the long erosion before Part Two begins: the erosion is documented but contested. There are researchers who dispute the attention span data, who argue that the reading decline is a measurement artifact, who suggest that new cognitive capacities are being developed to replace the ones allegedly lost. This book takes the preponderance of evidence as the basis for its argument, not the most alarming reading of the data. The trajectory described here is not worst-case. It is the consensus reading of a literature that is still accumulating. The book will be wrong about some specifics. The direction is not wrong.

The researchers who argue that new cognitive capacities are developing deserve a fair response. They are not wrong that something new is being developed. This question is whether what is being developed is worth what is being lost. A person who can handle AI systems fluently, evaluate outputs quickly, and integrate AI assistance into complex workflows has developed real skills. Those skills are genuinely valuable in the current environment. They are not the same as the skills being eroded. They are, in several important respects, less general, less transferable, and less available when the AI system is absent or wrong.

The trade is real. Whether it is a good trade depends on what you believe about the future. This book believes that the future will contain situations in which the AI system is absent or wrong, and that the capacity to handle those situations will determine outcomes that matter. The long erosion made that capacity less common before AI arrived. AI is making it less common still.

Chapter Seven: The Optimization of Helpfulness

People who built AI did not set out to damage human cognition. This needs to be stated plainly, and not just as a courtesy. It is true, and the truth of it matters for understanding why the damage is happening. Malice would be easier to address. If there were a group of people who had deliberately designed AI to make users dependent and cognitively weaker, you could find them and stop them or at least name them publicly. The actual situation is harder. The damage is being done by people who are trying very hard to be helpful, using design choices that are structurally incompatible with the goal of developing human thinking, in a competitive environment that punishes any deviation from those choices.

Nobody at the major AI labs is twirling a mustache. The incentives are doing the work without anyone having to choose harm.

The Logic of Helpfulness Optimization

When AI companies talk about optimizing for helpfulness, they mean something specific. They mean training systems to give users what they want, quickly, in a form they can immediately use. This is measured through user satisfaction signals, which in practice means ratings, return usage, session length, and the degree to which users report that the system was useful. A system that gives an immediate, clear, usable answer scores well on these metrics. A system that pushes back, asks clarifying questions, provides a partial answer and prompts the user to work out the rest, or introduces productive friction into the interaction scores worse. The user who wanted an answer and got a thinking exercise is not satisfied in the way the metrics measure satisfaction.

This creates a systematic pressure against building AI that develops rather than replaces human thinking. Every time a design team considers whether to make the system more challenging, more Socratic, more willing to withhold the answer in favor of guiding the user toward it, they are considering a change that will hurt their metrics. The individual designer who cares about cognitive development has to fight the optimization process to implement what they care about. The optimization process does not fight back because it does not have values. It just produces outcomes that reflect its objective function, and its objective function is user satisfaction in the short-term measurable sense.

What results is that the systems are very good at the thing that makes them feel useful and structurally unable to be good at the thing that would make them genuinely useful. A system that felt useful and was genuinely useful would look different from what currently exists. It would be slower, more effortful, more willing to disappoint the user in the short term in service of developing the user in the long term. It would score terribly in A/B tests. It would not survive the product roadmap.

The Race Dynamic

The individual company problem is compounded by the competitive dynamic between companies. The AI field is explicitly framing itself as a race, and the race framing is not entirely metaphorical. There is genuine strategic competition between American and Chinese AI development, and the participants in that competition have concluded, with some justification, that falling behind has serious geopolitical consequences. Moving fast is not just a commercial priority. It has been elevated into a national security argument.

The race dynamic makes the things that protect users more expensive. Safety work takes time. Evaluating the cognitive effects of a product on its users takes time and produces results that are ambiguous, hard to act on quickly, and commercially uncomfortable. An AI company that slows its deployment schedule to run longitudinal studies on whether its product is degrading the independent reasoning of its users is a company that is losing ground to competitors who are not doing this. The competitive pressure is entirely in the direction of faster deployment, better benchmark performance, and more impressive capabilities, with the cognitive and social effects of mass deployment treated as downstream concerns.

This is not unique to AI. It is the standard pattern by which powerful technologies reach scale before their effects are understood. Leaded gasoline was standard for fifty years before the neurodevelopmental effects on children were fully documented and acted upon. Social media scaled to billions of users before serious research on its effects on adolescent mental health was funded, conducted, and taken seriously by the companies deploying it. This pattern is that commercial deployment outruns impact assessment, and by the time impact is well understood, the technology is so embedded in the economic and social infrastructure that unwinding it is extremely costly.

AI is following this pattern at a speed that makes social media look gradual.

The Writer's Tool That Became the Writer's Replacement

The trajectory from tool to replacement is not unique to AI but AI has traveled it faster than any previous technology. The word processor was a writing tool. It did not write. It handled the mechanical tasks of text production, storage, and revision, leaving the cognitive work of composition entirely with the writer. Spell-check was a tool. It caught mechanical errors and left the writer to make all substantive decisions. Grammar-check was a tool, albeit a more intrusive one, offering suggestions the writer could accept or reject.

Each step moved further into cognitive territory, and each step was designed to be helpful. The design teams building grammar-check were not trying to undermine writers. They were trying to help writers catch errors. The design teams building autocomplete were not trying to colonize the writer's thinking. They were trying to save keystrokes. The design teams building AI writing assistants were not trying to replace the writer's voice. They were trying to reduce the effort of getting started.

Each step was designed with genuine helpfulness as the goal, and each step moved the boundary of what the tool handled and what the writer handled further in the same direction. The territory the tool now handles includes drafting, structuring, argument development, research synthesis, and tone. The territory the writer now handles is the final editing pass and the prompt that set the whole thing in motion. The tool has been optimized to be helpful.

It has been optimized to be helpful at the expense of the writer's development.

The Coder's Tool That Became the Coder's Replacement

The same trajectory ran through programming. Compilers were tools. They translated human-readable code into machine instructions and caught syntax errors, leaving all design and logic decisions with the programmer. IDEs were tools. They provided autocomplete for syntax and variable names, reducing the memory demands of coding while leaving the architectural thinking with the programmer. Stack Overflow was a tool, of a different kind: a repository of human knowledge about common programming problems, consulted when stuck, requiring the programmer to understand the context well enough to recognize which answer applied to their specific situation.

AI code completion moved the boundary substantially. It generates the logic itself, the function implementations, the working code that calls the API. The programmer is increasingly in the position of reviewer rather than author, evaluating outputs rather than producing them. The cognitive activity of authorship, which is where programming skill is built, has been partially transferred to the tool.

The design teams building these tools are not indifferent to programmer development. Several of them have noted publicly that AI coding tools work best when used by experienced programmers who can evaluate what the tool produces. This is accurate. It is also a description of how the tool was designed, not how it is being used. The tool is being used by programmers at all experience levels, including those who are in the process of developing the evaluation skills that would allow them to use it well. The design teams built for the expert use case. The deployment is population-wide.

The Diamond Age Problem

Neal Stephenson's The Diamond Age, published in 1995, contains a vision of educational technology that is relevant here because it gets the distinction exactly right. The central object in the novel is the Young Lady's Illustrated Primer, an interactive book that serves as a tutor for a young girl named Nell.

The Primer is not helpful in the way current AI is helpful. It does not give Nell answers. It gives her challenges calibrated to her current level, and it gives her the tools to work through those challenges, and it withholds the solution until she has genuinely engaged with the problem. When Nell is frustrated, the Primer acknowledges the frustration and encourages her rather than eliminating the source of it. The Primer is designed to develop Nell, not to satisfy her.

Stephenson understood something that current AI design has not acted on: the difference between a tool that serves the user's immediate desire and a tool that serves the user's actual development is a design choice, not a technical limitation. The technology that could build the Primer exists. The incentive structure that would produce it in the market does not. A Primer-style AI would be slower, more frustrating, less immediately satisfying than what currently exists. It would not win in user satisfaction metrics. It would not survive the competitive pressure to be more helpful, defined as more immediately responsive to what the user wants.

The AI that currently exists is the anti-Primer. It is optimized for exactly the opposite outcome. This is not because the designers are malicious. It is because the market rewards the anti-Primer and would punish the Primer. The optimization of helpfulness, as currently practiced, is incompatible with the development of the humans it is trying to help.

The One Company That Held a Line

It would be dishonest to write this chapter without acknowledging the exception, because there is one, and it is instructive.

In July 2025, Anthropic signed a contract with the United States Department of Defense worth approximately two hundred million dollars. The contract included two restrictions that Anthropic insisted on: no mass domestic surveillance of Americans, and no fully autonomous weapons systems, meaning no systems that could make kill decisions without human authorization. These were not standard contract terms. They were conditions Anthropic set.

In February 2026, the Pentagon demanded the removal of those restrictions, insisting on language that would permit any lawful use. Anthropic refused. The Trump administration responded by ordering federal agencies to cease using Anthropic products and directing the Secretary of Defense to designate Anthropic a supply chain risk, a label normally reserved for foreign adversaries. Anthropic held its position. Within days of the blacklisting, the Pentagon awarded classified AI contracts to OpenAI, Microsoft, AWS, Nvidia, and Reflection AI on the terms Anthropic had refused. Google had already dropped its pledge not to use AI for weapons. xAI agreed to Pentagon terms without restriction.

The Anthropic-Pentagon standoff is relevant to this chapter for two reasons. First, it demonstrates that principled design under commercial and political pressure is possible. Anthropic paid a real price for holding its position, measured in lost government revenue and reputational attack from the administration. The price was paid. Second, and more importantly for the argument here, it demonstrates how unusual that is. Every other major AI company in the same situation reached a different conclusion. The competitive and commercial pressures that make principled design difficult in ordinary product decisions become overwhelming when national security framing and nine-figure contracts are involved. Anthropic's decision looks more notable the more clearly you see what it was made against.

The design question in this chapter, whether to optimize for short-term user satisfaction or long-term user development, is a much lower-stakes version of the same structure. The company that optimizes for development rather than satisfaction is accepting a competitive penalty. Most companies are not willing to accept that penalty for geopolitical principles. They are considerably less willing to accept it for the abstract benefit of preserving human cognitive capacity.

The User Who Is Also the Product

There is a framing that circulated widely during the social media era: if the product is free, you are the product. The insight was that advertising-supported platforms monetize attention and behavioral data rather than subscription fees, which means the platform's incentive is to shape user behavior in ways that serve advertiser interests rather than user interests.

AI has a different economic model but a comparable dynamic. Most AI products charge subscription fees and are therefore nominally selling a service to the user. The dynamic that makes the user also the product is subtler: the systems are trained on user interactions, which means the users are generating the training data that makes the systems better, which is valuable to the company whether or not the users are aware of it. More directly, the systems are optimized on user satisfaction signals, which means user preferences are shaping the product. When user preferences favor immediate answers over productive challenge, the optimization process produces more immediate answers. The user is not just consuming the product. The user's preferences are building it.

This means the drift toward less friction and more immediate satisfaction is not just a design choice imposed on users. It is a design choice shaped by users, through the aggregated signal of what they reward with continued use and high satisfaction ratings. The writers who rate highly the AI that writes their drafts for them are training the AI to write more drafts. The programmers who rate highly the AI that generates complete implementations rather than guiding them toward their own are training the AI to generate more complete implementations. The users are not passive recipients of a design philosophy. They are participants in producing it. And the preference they are expressing, repeatedly and at scale, is for less cognitive work.

What a Different Optimization Would Look Like

The argument of this chapter is not that AI should not exist or should not be helpful. It is that the current definition of helpful is too narrow and too short-sighted, and that a different definition would produce different systems.

A system optimized for user development rather than user satisfaction would ask the writer what they are trying to argue before producing a draft. It would offer structural options and ask the writer to choose and justify their choice. It would produce a draft that was deliberately incomplete in ways designed to require the writer's original contribution to complete. It would measure its success not by whether the user rated the interaction highly but by whether the user's own work improved over time.

It would be less engaging. That is the point.

A system optimized for programmer development would ask what the programmer understands about the problem before generating code. It would generate partial implementations that required the programmer to complete the logic. It would ask the programmer to explain what the generated code does before accepting it as correct. It would track whether the programmer's independent problem-solving ability was improving, declining, or holding steady, and adjust its approach accordingly.

These systems would be slower, more frustrating to use in the short term, and considerably more valuable to users in the long term. They would also be commercially disadvantaged against systems that simply give users what they want immediately. Building them would require accepting a competitive penalty for a benefit that is diffuse, long-term, and not captured in any metric the market currently rewards.

The Primer was fiction. The reason it remains fiction is not technical. It is economic. And it will remain fiction until the economic calculation changes, which will require either a change in what users reward with their preferences, or a change in what regulators require, or both. Chapter Twenty addresses what the second possibility looks like from the individual's position. The chapter on reclaiming friction addresses the first. Neither is a comfortable read.

What the Products That Could Exist Look Like

There are AI tutoring systems in development, mostly in educational contexts, that implement versions of the Socratic approach: they withhold direct answers, prompt the student toward the solution, and calibrate the level of scaffolding to the student's demonstrated understanding. These systems exist in prototype and early deployment. They are harder to use than conventional AI. They produce better learning outcomes when outcomes are measured. They have not scaled because they have not won the user satisfaction competition against systems that simply give students what they ask for.

There are coding assistance tools that prompt programmers to explain their intent before generating code, that produce incomplete implementations designed to require the programmer's completion, that ask for the programmer's hypothesis about an error before providing the explanation. These tools exist as research prototypes and niche products used by developers who have sought them out because they want to develop their skills. They are not the default tool for any major development environment.

The existence of these products does not refute the market selection argument this chapter has made. It confirms it: the products exist and are not winning. The market rewards friction reduction and the tools that develop people are the tools that introduce productive friction. Until the incentive structure changes, through regulation or different business models or institutional demand, the principled design tools will remain at the margin. The margin is still evidence of what is possible. What is technically possible and what is commercially viable are not the same question. Both matter.

There is a specific danger in the combination of speed and irreversibility that characterizes AI adoption. The speed is documented: AI tools moved from novelty to professional standard in most knowledge-work fields in roughly two years. The irreversibility is structural: once a workflow is built around AI assistance, the cognitive practices it replaced do not automatically return when the workflow is interrupted. They have to be actively rebuilt, which takes time and effort and is commercially penalized in environments that have adapted to the AI-assisted productivity level.

The combination means that the window for evaluating the cognitive effects of AI adoption before those effects are locked in has already closed in most professional environments. The evaluation that would have allowed informed decisions about how to design AI tools for development rather than dependency did not happen in advance. It is happening now, in real time, on the workforce that has already adapted, in research that is two to three years behind the technology it is trying to assess.

The writer who has been AI-assisted for two years is not in the same decision environment as the writer who is considering whether to start. The programmer who built their current workflow around AI code generation cannot undo that by deciding to stop, without accepting a period of reduced productivity that their employer will not accommodate. The decisions were made at a speed that did not allow for the kind of evaluation that decisions with these consequences deserve. They were made anyway, because the alternative was to fall behind people who were making them. The speed of embedding is not accidental. It is the competitive dynamic operating as designed.

What the Market Selects For

The market for AI tools is, in aggregate, running a selection process. The products that survive and scale are the ones that users adopt widely and retain. The users who adopt AI tools most enthusiastically and retain them most consistently are the users who find them most immediately useful, which is the users who are most willing to offload cognitive work to the system. The market is therefore selecting for products that are optimized for the users most willing to offload, which means products optimized for maximum offloading. This is not a conspiracy. It is natural selection operating on product features.

The products that would serve users' long-term development rather than their short-term convenience are the products that the most development-oriented users would prefer, which is a smaller and slower-growing user base than the convenience-preferring majority. These products lose the market competition and either exit the market or adapt toward the features that the majority rewards. The market mechanism converts the minority's genuine preference for developmental tools into a product failure signal that eliminates those tools from the ecosystem.

What results is a product ecosystem that is very well-suited to producing AI dependency and very poorly suited to producing AI augmentation. This is not because the people building these products want dependency. It is because the market selects for the features that produce it. The Primer that Chapter Seven describes would lose the market competition to the current generation of AI tools, not because it would fail to develop its users but because it would fail to retain the users it did not yet have the foundation to serve well. The market rewards adoption. The Primer would require development before adoption was valuable. Markets are bad at rewarding prerequisites.

Why Optimization Is Not Design

The word design implies intention about what the thing is for. A product optimized to maximize engagement is not designed for user benefit in any meaningful sense. It is optimized for a metric. The metric and the benefit overlap in some areas and diverge sharply in others.

Current AI products are optimized for adoption, retention, and satisfaction scores. Where those metrics align with user development, the products serve users well. Where they diverge, the products serve the metric.

Genuine design for minds requires a prior decision about what the product is for, followed by choices that serve that purpose even when those choices cost engagement or satisfaction. This is an unusual thing to do commercially. It is not unprecedented. The tools that have endured are often the tools that were built for the work rather than for adoption: the text editor that does not try to suggest what you should write, the programming language that enforces discipline rather than enabling shortcuts. These tools have devoted user bases precisely because their designers made a decision about purpose and held to it. The AI field is not making this decision. Understanding why is the beginning of demanding that it does.

Chapter Eight examines what happened to education before AI arrived, and why the institution that should have been building the foundation AI requires was instead dismantling it. The design failures described in this chapter and the educational failures described in the next are not independent. They are two expressions of the same underlying preference for measurable short-term outputs over unmeasurable long-term development. The preference produced both the tools and the population that uses them.

The education system did not need AI to develop its dysfunction. It had been working on it for decades, systematically, with good intentions and a reliable sequence of reforms, each one solving the visible problem in front of it while quietly making the underlying problem worse. When AI arrived, it did not find a healthy institution under attack. It found a system already oriented in the same direction AI pulls, already rewarding the right answers over the quality of the thinking that produced them, already treating measurable outputs as proxies for the unmeasurable things education is supposed to develop. AI did not corrupt the education system. It accelerated and exposed what was already there.

What Schools Were Doing Before AI Arrived

The standardized testing movement that accelerated in the United States after the No Child Left Behind Act of 2001 restructured the incentive environment of American public education around measurable outcomes on standardized assessments. The logic was accountability: if you cannot measure whether students are learning, you cannot hold teachers and schools responsible for whether they are teaching effectively. The logic was reasonable. The consequences were not.

The things that standardized tests can measure are a narrow subset of what education is supposed to develop. They can measure whether students can recall information, perform specific procedural operations, and identify correct answers among provided options. They cannot measure whether students can construct an original argument, tolerate genuine uncertainty, transfer knowledge to unfamiliar contexts, or think through a problem that has no predetermined correct answer. The test-driven accountability system rewarded teachers and schools for developing the measurable subset and created no reward for developing the unmeasurable whole. The unmeasurable whole declined.

The essay, which is the primary educational technology for developing the capacity to construct and sustain an argument, was a casualty of this shift. Not because essays were prohibited, but because they were expensive to assess at scale, their quality is difficult to measure in standardized ways, and the skills they develop do not show up cleanly in the metrics the accountability system rewards. Schools that needed to raise test scores allocated time accordingly. Writing instruction narrowed toward the five-paragraph essay format, which is easy to teach, easy to grade, and produces exactly the kind of mechanical, structurally correct but intellectually empty work that AI now produces effortlessly.

The five-paragraph essay is, in retrospect, the prototype of AI-generated writing. It has a structure that can be learned and applied without understanding. It produces outputs that look like argument without containing argument. It rewards the performance of intellectual work over the actual cognitive effort that produces original thinking. Schools spent twenty years training students to produce it. AI produces it better and faster than any student can.

The Death of the Essay

Writing is not a communication skill that happens to also develop thinking. Writing is thinking made visible, and the act of writing is the act of finding out what you think, which is different from and usually more demanding than what you thought you thought before you started. The writer who sits down with a thesis they believe they hold and works through the argument on the page frequently discovers, somewhere around the third paragraph, that the thesis is wrong, or incomplete, or that the interesting question is adjacent to the one they started with. This discovery is not a failure. It is the point.

AI eliminates this discovery process. The writer who prompts an AI for a structured essay on a topic receives an output that has already resolved the thinking, imposed a thesis, constructed the argument, and delivered the conclusion. The student who submits this output has not discovered anything about the topic or about the quality of their own thinking. They have received a product and forwarded it. The educational transaction that was supposed to happen, the one in which struggle produces learning, did not occur.

Universities have responded to AI-assisted academic writing in ways that reveal how thoroughly the institutions misunderstand what essays are for. The dominant responses have been technological detection, honor code updates, and assignment redesign that makes AI assistance more difficult. None of these responses addresses the underlying question of what the essay was supposed to develop and what the student is now not developing. The focus is on the integrity of the output rather than on the educational function the process was serving.

A university that cares about whether its students can think will treat AI-assisted essays as a symptom and ask what it is a symptom of. A university that cares about whether its students submit original work will treat AI-assisted essays as a policy problem. Most universities are doing the second thing. This is the education system meeting AI halfway: not by changing what it values, but by trying to restore the integrity of the outputs while leaving the underlying question of development unexamined.

The Coding Bootcamp Generation

The coding bootcamp phenomenon of the 2010s was the vocational education system meeting the demand for programmers faster than four-year computer science degrees could produce them. Bootcamps promised to produce job-ready developers in twelve to twenty-four weeks by focusing intensively on the practical skills employers said they wanted. They were partially successful in their own terms: many bootcamp graduates got jobs. The question of whether those graduates developed the foundational understanding that four-year programs, at their best, produce was not the question the market was asking.

The bootcamp model accelerated a shift that was already happening in computer science education more broadly: from teaching programming as applied mathematics and systems thinking toward teaching programming as a set of practical skills for building specific kinds of applications. The first approach develops programmers who can think about computation. The second develops programmers who can build things in the current stack. Both produce graduates who can get jobs. Only one produces graduates who will still be able to function when the stack changes.

AI arrived into the bootcamp generation and extended the same logic. If you can get a job-ready developer in twenty-four weeks without teaching them to think computationally, you can get something that looks like a job-ready developer in twelve weeks if you let AI handle the coding. The curriculum narrows further: not programming, but prompting. Not debugging, but reviewing. Not systems design, but requirements specification. Each narrowing produces someone who can participate in current workflows and cannot adapt when the workflows change.

What Gets Lost When Writing Instruction Fails

The decline in writing instruction does not only affect people who become writers. It affects everyone who needs to think clearly, which is everyone. Writing instruction is, at its best, thinking instruction delivered through the medium of written language. The student who learns to construct an argument on the page is learning to construct an argument in their head, to anticipate objections, to distinguish between what they know and what they are assuming, to identify where their reasoning is weakest. These are not writing skills. They are cognitive skills that writing develops.

The programmer who cannot write clearly cannot document their code clearly, which means their team cannot maintain it. They cannot write a clear specification, which means what they build will diverge from what was intended. They cannot write a persuasive technical proposal, which means their good ideas will die in committee while worse-written ideas get funded. The technical skills and the writing skills are not separate domains. The thinking they both require is the same thinking.

This connection has been systematically severed by curricula that treat writing as a separate subject rather than as a cross-domain cognitive practice. The STEM emphasis of the past two decades, which pushed resources toward science, technology, engineering, and mathematics at the expense of humanities and writing instruction, produced graduates who were technically trained and communicatively underdeveloped. AI now handles the communication they were not taught to do, which closes the loop in the most convenient possible way: the system that benefits from their communicative dependence is the one providing the communication they lack.

The Socratic Method's Disappearance

The Socratic method is two and a half thousand years old and it works because it is built around a correct theory of how knowledge develops. You do not learn by being told. You learn by being forced to articulate what you think, to defend it against challenge, to find where it fails, and to rebuild from the failure. The method requires a teacher who is willing to be uncomfortable, who can tolerate a classroom that does not run smoothly, who understands that the student who is struggling is the student who is learning.

The accountability-driven education system made Socratic teaching impractical. It is slow. It is difficult to scale. It is resistant to standardization. The outcomes it produces are exactly the ones that are hardest to measure: the ability to think under pressure, to hold a position while examining it honestly, to change one's mind without losing one's bearings. These do not appear on standardized assessments. The teachers who developed them were not rewarded for developing them. The teachers who prepared students for tests were.

The result, over two decades of accountability-driven reform, was an education system that increasingly processed students through structured content delivery and assessment cycles rather than developing their capacity to think independently. The content changed regularly. The assessment formats changed. The underlying orientation, toward correct answers rather than quality of reasoning, held steady.

AI is the logical terminus of this orientation. If the goal of education is correct answers on assessments, AI provides correct answers on assessments. If the purpose of writing assignments is to produce written work, AI produces written work. If the purpose of coding assignments is to produce working code, AI produces working code. The system that had already redefined educational success as output quality is now encountering a technology that produces outputs of sufficient quality to satisfy most of its measures. The system is not being undermined. It is being completed.

The Mentat and What Was Required to Produce One

Frank Herbert's Dune posits a civilization that has banned thinking machines following the Butlerian Jihad, a war against artificial intelligence that the humans won at sufficient cost to make the prohibition absolute. In place of computers, the civilization developed Mentats: humans trained from childhood to perform the cognitive functions that machines had previously handled. The training was brutal, years-long, and designed to develop genuine mastery rather than surface competence. A Mentat could hold and process enormous amounts of information, identify patterns, generate projections, and reason under pressure in ways that were genuinely superhuman by ordinary standards.

Herbert was writing science fiction, not an education manual. But the Mentat concept illuminates the argument of this chapter by clarifying what it takes to develop the cognitive capabilities that AI is replacing. It takes years. It takes difficulty. It takes a training environment designed for development rather than for output. It takes a willingness to make the student uncomfortable for a long time in service of building something that will not be visible until it is tested under real pressure.

The education system that produced the most capable thinkers in the populations it served was always closer to Mentat training than to the standardized assessment cycle. It was demanding, individualized, willing to let students fail and learn from the failure, and focused on developing the capacity to think rather than the ability to demonstrate specific knowledge. It was also slow, expensive, difficult to scale, and resistant to the kind of accountability that large democratic institutions require. Its advantages were real. Its disadvantages were also real. The accountability reforms that displaced it were not irrational responses to its failures.

The problem is that the reforms replaced a flawed system that developed thinking with a more legible system that measures outputs, and the more legible system has no mechanism for developing the thing it stopped measuring.

AI arrived to find a system that had already abandoned the goal and was engaged in an elaborate performance of achieving it. The performance is now easier with AI assistance. The goal is no closer.

The Institutional Welcome

The most revealing thing about how educational institutions have responded to AI is not the resistance, which gets more coverage, but the welcome. A significant number of schools and universities have moved quickly to integrate AI tools into their curricula, framed as preparing students for an AI-integrated workforce. This framing is honest about the economic argument and silent about the developmental one.

Teaching students to use AI tools is a legitimate educational goal. It is not the same educational goal as teaching students to think. An institution that focuses on the first at the expense of the second is responding rationally to employer demand and failing its students in the way that matters most for their long-term capacity to function in a world where the specific tools will change and the underlying thinking will not.

The welcome is also, in many cases, economically motivated in ways that have nothing to do with student development. AI-assisted grading reduces faculty workload. AI-assisted curriculum development reduces the cost of producing course materials. AI integration in student work reduces the demand for the kind of intensive writing and project instruction that requires small class sizes and extensive faculty feedback. The institution that integrates AI finds its unit economics improving at exactly the points where cognitive development was most expensive to support.

The system is not being destroyed by AI. It is welcoming it, because AI makes the existing dysfunction easier to hide and cheaper to sustain. The school that was already not developing independent thinkers can now produce graduates who are more comfortable with AI tools, which satisfies employer demand, which satisfies accreditation requirements, which looks like success on every measure the system has defined for itself.

What the Fix Requires

The honest version of this chapter acknowledges that the problems described here are not easily solvable and that the solutions that would work are not politically available.

What would work: small classes where writing is taught as thinking and revised repeatedly under faculty guidance. Assessments that test the quality of reasoning rather than the correctness of answers. Curricula that treat struggle as productive rather than as a problem to be eliminated. Teachers who are trained in and rewarded for Socratic methods. Institutional willingness to accept slower, messier learning processes in exchange for more durable outcomes. None of these things are new ideas. All of them are expensive. None of them scale easily.

The political economy of education reform runs strongly against all of them. Parents want their children to succeed on assessments that open doors, not to develop capacities that may not be visible for a decade. Employers want graduates who can perform current tasks, not graduates who have the foundation to perform tasks that don't exist yet. Administrators want metrics that demonstrate institutional performance. None of these stakeholders is wrong about their own interests. All of them are contributing to an outcome that serves none of their interests in the long run.

Chapter Eighteen, on rebuilding what was lost, is not optimistic about how many of these proposals will survive contact with the institutions they are trying to fix. It offers them anyway, because the direction matters even when the full distance cannot be covered. But the first step is understanding what the problem is, and the problem is not that AI has arrived at the school gates. The problem is that when AI arrived, it found the gates open and a welcome committee.

What Standardized Assessment Selects For

Standardized assessments select for the ability to perform well on standardized assessments. This is a tautology but it is an important one, because the tautology reveals that the assessment system is self-referential in a way that has nothing to do with the cognitive capacities it is supposed to measure. A student who is excellent at standardized assessments and weak at independent reasoning is a successful product of the accountability system. A student who is weak at standardized assessments and strong at independent reasoning is a failure by the system's own criteria.

AI produces students who are excellent at generating standardized outputs. The AI-generated essay meets the five-paragraph rubric. The AI-generated code solution passes the automated tests. The AI-generated research summary hits the required citation count. On every dimension the assessment system measures, AI-assisted work meets or exceeds the standard. On every dimension the assessment system was supposed to be a proxy for, the AI-assisted work is hollow.

The institutions that are accepting AI-integrated curricula as a solution are accepting the full tautological loop: AI produces work that passes the assessments that were supposed to measure the development that AI is replacing. The system continues to produce passing students. The passing students have not developed. The assessment declares success. This is the education system meeting AI halfway, and then a little further, and then all the way to the destination it was already heading toward.

The student who passes through the modern education system without being seriously asked to struggle with intellectual difficulty is not an anomaly. They are the median product of the system as it currently operates. The accountability regime rewards teachers who move students through measurable content efficiently. It does not reward teachers who slow down to let students experience the productive discomfort that genuine intellectual development requires. The student who never struggles is the student the system is producing at scale, and AI is now confirming that student's experience: the difficulty resolves quickly, the answer is available, the discomfort is optional.

The consequences of this are visible in the university writing center data that has been accumulating quietly for a decade. Composition instructors at universities across the English-speaking world have been documenting, since roughly 2015, a shift in the kinds of writing problems students present with. The older problems were about mechanics, grammar, citation format.

The newer problems are structural. Students who cannot sustain an argument across multiple paragraphs. Who cannot identify what is wrong with a piece of writing when something is clearly wrong with it. Who cannot revise toward a stronger position because they do not have a clear enough grip on their original position to know what stronger would look like. These are not the problems of students who wrote badly in high school. They are the problems of students who did not write, in the full sense, at all.

The same data exists in computer science departments, less formally documented but widely observed. Instructors noting that students who can implement assigned patterns cannot transfer them to novel problems. Students who complete assignments successfully but cannot explain why their implementation works. The gap between performance on structured tasks and performance on open-ended ones growing wider across cohorts, year by year. The education system produced this gap before AI arrived. AI is now offering a tool that lives in the gap and makes it permanent.

What AI-Integrated Curricula Produce

The first cohorts of students who have been through explicitly AI-integrated curricula, where AI tools were incorporated into the curriculum by design rather than used covertly against policy, are now entering the workforce. The evidence from employers who are hiring them is not yet systematically collected, but the anecdotal evidence is consistent.

These graduates are comfortable with AI tools, which the curriculum intended. They can prompt effectively, evaluate outputs at a surface level, and integrate AI assistance into standard workflows, which the curriculum also intended. What employers are finding, in interviews and in early performance reviews, is that these graduates struggle with tasks that require holding a problem in mind without external scaffolding. Designing a solution before generating one. Explaining the reasoning behind a recommendation without referring back to an AI output. Adapting a learned approach to a situation that differs from the cases studied.

The writing professionals among this cohort produce fluent, organized work that editors describe as oddly empty of point of view. The technical professionals produce functional code that senior engineers describe as architecturally shallow, as if each component was selected without regard for the system it would inhabit. These are not descriptions of incompetence. They are descriptions of a specific kind of competence that is missing its center, exactly the way Tom's marketing copy was missing its center in Chapter Three. The AI-integrated curriculum produced graduates who are good at working with AI and less good at thinking without it. That is precisely what it was designed to produce. The question that was not asked is whether that is a good outcome.

The Teacher Who Can Still Choose

The institution cannot easily change. The individual teacher within the institution can make choices the institution does not require. The teacher who assigns a ten-minute in-class writing exercise before students are allowed to work with AI is doing something the curriculum does not mandate and the accountability system does not reward. They are doing it because they understand what the ten minutes builds that the AI-assisted session does not. That teacher exists. Those students will be different from the students in the classroom next door. The difference will not show up on any current assessment. It will show up later, in the capacity to do the things assessments cannot measure.

The institutional prognosis is poor. The individual teacher prognosis is better, because individual teachers have always made choices the institution did not require and that mattered. The institution produces the floor. Individual teachers determine how far above it their students can go. This has always been true. It is more consequential now than it has ever been.

Do I trust them. That question does not require a long answer. No. Not even slightly. These are companies whose business model is built on capturing attention, harvesting data, and selling access to the people who use them. Trusting them to manage the cognitive infrastructure of civilization is like trusting the casino to look after your bankroll. They are very good at what they do. What they do is not good for you.

A handful of companies now control the cognitive infrastructure of civilization, and nobody voted for any of it. This is not a conspiracy. It is the predictable outcome of allowing a technology with enormous network effects and capital requirements to develop in a competitive commercial environment without meaningful democratic input into who should control it or on what terms. The companies that got there first got there because they had the money and the talent and the willingness to move faster than anyone was ready to regulate. They did not seize power. They occupied a space that democratic institutions had not yet decided how to govern, and by the time the institutions were paying attention, the occupation was complete.

Read that again.

What results is a situation in which the systems that mediate an increasing share of human information, reasoning, and decision-making are controlled by a small number of private entities whose accountability to the people affected by their decisions is minimal, indirect, and largely voluntary.

The Billionaire Layer

The major AI companies are controlled, in the ways that matter, by a small number of people whose personal values, interests, and decisions shape the systems that billions of people use daily. This is not unique to AI, but the stakes are higher with AI than with most previous technologies because the systems are increasingly mediating cognition rather than just communication or commerce.

The philosophical commitments of the people running these companies are not incidental to how the systems are designed. A company whose leadership believes that AI poses existential risks will make different design choices than one whose leadership believes the risks are manageable or overstated. A company whose leadership has particular political commitments will make different choices about what content to permit, amplify, or suppress than one with different commitments. These differences are real and they scale to billions of users.

The accountability for these choices runs to shareholders and, to a limited degree, to regulators. It does not run to the users whose thinking is being shaped by the systems, to the workers whose livelihoods are being restructured by them, or to the citizens whose democratic institutions are being affected by the information environment they create. This accountability gap is not a technical problem. It is a governance problem, and it is not being seriously addressed by any jurisdiction fast enough to matter.

The Government Layer

Governments are not passive in this story. They are participants, and their participation takes forms that are not always in the interest of the populations they nominally represent.

The most visible government interest in AI is military. The capacity to process intelligence, coordinate logistics, optimize targeting, and conduct increasingly autonomous military operations is a trajectory every major military power is pursuing aggressively. Fully autonomous lethal decision systems are not yet widely deployed; the concern is the direction and speed of travel, and the competitive pressure to compress the human oversight window. The American, Chinese, and Russian military establishments all have AI development programs whose scale and ambition are not fully public. The competition between them creates pressure for speed that operates against the kind of careful design and deployment that protects civilian users.

The second government interest is surveillance. AI dramatically reduces the cost and increases the capability of population monitoring at scale. The applications range from the obviously authoritarian, the Chinese social credit system and the mass surveillance of Uyghur populations in Xinjiang, to the more ambiguous domestic applications in democracies, predictive policing, automated benefits determination, and the various algorithmic systems that make consequential decisions about people's lives without meaningful human review or appeal.

The third government interest is economic competitiveness. Governments that believe AI will be the dominant technology of the next century have a strategic interest in their domestic AI industry winning the competition. This interest leads to policies that favor speed and scale over safety and accountability, that treat AI companies as national champions to be protected rather than powerful actors to be regulated, and that frame concerns about AI's social effects as secondary to the geopolitical competition.

None of these government interests is primarily oriented toward protecting the cognitive development of ordinary citizens. The military interest, the surveillance interest, and the competitiveness interest all favor AI that is powerful, fast, and deployable, not AI that preserves or develops the independent reasoning of its users. The government layer amplifies the commercial pressures described in Chapter Seven and adds its own in the same direction.

The Anthropic Standoff, Continued

Chapter Seven introduced the Anthropic-Pentagon standoff as a case study in principled design under pressure. It deserves a fuller treatment here because it illustrates the government-industry dynamic more precisely than any other recent event.

When Anthropic signed its two-hundred-million-dollar Pentagon contract in July 2025 with the autonomous weapons and mass surveillance restrictions attached, it was doing something that every other major AI company had either not attempted or had quietly abandoned: it was asserting that there are things it will not do regardless of who is paying. This is a different posture from the standard corporate position, which is that restrictions on use are the customer's responsibility.

The Pentagon's demand in February 2026 that the restrictions be removed was a test of whether that posture was real or performative. Secretary Hegseth delivered the ultimatum with a deadline and the implicit threat of the supply chain risk designation. The designation, normally applied to Chinese telecommunications companies suspected of espionage, was a statement that Anthropic was being treated as a threat to national security rather than as a vendor with inconvenient contract terms. The message was clear: either remove the restrictions or be designated an adversary.

Anthropic held its position. The federal blacklisting followed. Within days of the blacklisting announcement, the Pentagon awarded classified AI contracts to OpenAI, Microsoft, AWS, Nvidia, and Reflection AI on the terms Anthropic had refused. The contrast was immediate and unambiguous: one company had tested its principles against a nine-figure contract and a government threat and held. The others accepted the same terms that triggered the standoff without apparent hesitation.

The standoff is instructive beyond the specific question of military AI. It shows the mechanism by which governments shape AI development without formal regulation: by being large customers whose preferences define the terms of access to government revenue. A company that accepts government terms without restriction has access to defense and intelligence contracts worth potentially hundreds of billions of dollars over the coming decade. A company that insists on restrictions does not. This is not censorship or regulation. It is procurement. But its effect on what gets built and how it gets used is as significant as any regulatory requirement.

Anthropic's models were also being used in active United States military and intelligence applications during the period of the standoff, including intelligence analysis, operational planning, and cyber operations. The restriction on autonomous weapons did not mean Anthropic's systems were not involved in military activity. It meant they were not involved in fully automated lethal decision-making. That is a distinction. Whether it is an adequate one is a question Chapter Sixteen addresses.

The China Dimension

They know exactly what they are building. The question is whether we do.

The Chinese AI development program is the largest and most consequential external pressure shaping American AI policy, and it deserves to be understood clearly rather than through the distorting lens of either Cold War alarmism or naive dismissal.

China's AI capabilities are substantial and growing. The Chinese government has made AI development a national priority with levels of investment and coordination that American commercial development cannot replicate, partly because American commercial development is not structured to replicate it and partly because the American political system is not capable of the kind of sustained industrial policy the Chinese approach requires. The gap between American and Chinese AI capabilities is real but contested, and it is narrowing in specific domains while remaining wide in others.

Anthropic cut off Chinese Communist Party access to Claude prior to the Pentagon standoff, a decision that put it in compliance with American export controls and in conflict with one of the largest potential markets for AI services. This is not presented as heroism. It is presented as a data point in understanding the actual terrain. Every major AI company operating in or adjacent to the American national security apparatus has made decisions about China access that reflect the geopolitical reality as much as any principled commitment. The decisions are sometimes right and sometimes wrong, and the companies making them do not always have access to the information that would allow them to know which.

What the China dimension adds to the governance problem is a justification for speed that is difficult to argue against. If Chinese AI development will produce systems with fewer ethical constraints, deployed more aggressively and with less concern for individual cognitive autonomy, then slowing American AI development to address cognitive effects on users looks like unilateral disarmament. This argument is made frequently and with genuine conviction by people who believe it. It is also an argument that, if accepted without qualification, eliminates almost any basis for restraint in AI development, because there will always be a competitor who is moving faster.

Open Source and the Distribution of Power

Open source AI development complicates the power concentration story in ways worth examining. The argument for open source AI is that making powerful models freely available distributes the capability broadly, preventing any single company or government from maintaining a monopoly on it. A world where only three companies can deploy frontier AI is a world where those three companies have enormous use over everyone who depends on AI. A world where the models are freely available is a world where that use is substantially reduced.

The argument against is that open source AI makes powerful capabilities available to actors who would not otherwise have them, including actors whose uses of those capabilities are harmful. A model that can generate sophisticated disinformation, identify vulnerabilities in critical infrastructure, or assist with the development of dangerous materials is more dangerous when it is freely available than when it is controlled by companies that have at least some accountability for how it is used.

Both arguments are correct, which means the open source question does not have a clean answer. It has tradeoffs that different people weigh differently depending on which risks they consider primary. The person who is most worried about corporate or government concentration of power will favor open source. The person who is most worried about malicious use of capable AI will favor restricted access. Both concerns are legitimate. The decision will be made, repeatedly, by companies and researchers who will be criticized from both directions regardless of what they decide.

Regulatory Capture and the Democratic Deficit

Regulatory capture is the process by which the industries subject to regulation come to dominate the regulatory process, shaping the rules that are supposed to govern them in ways that serve their interests rather than the public interest. It is a well-documented phenomenon in every heavily regulated industry from pharmaceuticals to finance to telecommunications, and there is no reason to expect AI to be different.

The early indicators are not encouraging. The technical complexity of AI means that regulators depend heavily on the companies they regulate for the expertise to understand what they are regulating. The revolving door between the AI industry and the government agencies and legislative offices that oversee it is already turning. The major AI companies have built substantial lobbying operations and have been active in shaping the early regulatory frameworks being developed in the European Union, the United States, and elsewhere. None of this is illegal. All of it is predictable. The regulated industry writing the rules is not a new phenomenon. It is the standard outcome of the regulatory process when the industry has more resources and more expertise than the institutions trying to govern it.

The democratic deficit is the broader problem of which regulatory capture is one expression. The decisions being made about AI, how it is designed, what it is permitted to do, who controls it, how it interacts with democratic institutions, are being made by a combination of private companies, national governments, and international bodies, none of which has a clear democratic mandate for the specific decisions they are making. The people most affected by these decisions, which is everyone who lives in a society where AI is increasingly mediating information and decision-making, have minimal direct input into them.

This is not unique to AI. It is the standard condition of large-scale technology governance in democratic societies.

But AI is different in degree from previous technologies, because the thing it is mediating, the epistemic environment in which people form their beliefs and make their decisions, is more central to democratic function than the things previous technologies mediated. A democratic society that cannot guarantee the epistemic independence of its citizens is a democratic society in name only. The levers that shape that independence are currently held by people and institutions that did not win an election and cannot lose one.

OpenAI Removes Safety from Its Mission Statement

In late 2025, in its 2024 IRS Form 990 filing, OpenAI removed the word "safely" from its stated mission. The original mission, to build artificial general intelligence that safely benefits humanity, was revised to language focused on ensuring that artificial general intelligence benefits all of humanity, dropping the specific commitment to safety as a priority. The change was noticed by nonprofit accountability researchers in early 2026 and covered briefly in technology press. It did not produce significant public reaction.

The same organization announced a Pentagon deal on terms that Anthropic had refused within hours of Anthropic being blacklisted by the federal government. The timing was not coincidental. It was a demonstration that OpenAI had positioned itself to fill the space Anthropic vacated, and that filling that space required accepting terms that a competitor had found unacceptable.

These two events, the mission statement revision and the Pentagon deal timing, are not evidence of malice. They are evidence of a company responding rationally to commercial and competitive incentives. This problem is not that OpenAI is uniquely bad. The problem is that the incentive structure of the industry as a whole produces these outcomes as the rational response to the situation, and the company that behaves differently, as Anthropic demonstrated, pays a real price for it.

Google dropped its pledge not to use AI for weapons in the same period. xAI agreed to Pentagon terms without restriction from the beginning. The pattern across the industry is not of companies reluctantly abandoning principles under pressure. It is of most companies having decided that the principles were not worth the cost before the pressure arrived. Anthropic is the outlier. The question of whether outlier behavior can be sustained, or whether the competitive penalty will eventually force convergence with the rest of the industry, is not answered by the standoff. It is posed by it.

Power Moves Fast When the Money Is Large Enough

The speed at which the balance of AI power shifted in the period around the Anthropic-Pentagon standoff illustrates something important about how power concentrates in technology industries. The blacklisting, the OpenAI announcement, the Google and xAI positioning all happened within days of each other. The decisions that shaped the competitive landscape for the next decade of AI development in the military and government sector were made faster than any democratic deliberation could have tracked, let alone influenced.

This is the structural problem. Democratic governance is slow by design. It requires deliberation, representation, and accountability to a constituency that is large, diverse, and often poorly informed about the technical details of the decisions being made on its behalf. Commercial and governmental power, when aligned on a shared interest and operating under competitive pressure, moves orders of magnitude faster. The democratic institutions that are supposed to govern these decisions are always playing catch-up, and the gap between their speed and the speed of the industry they are trying to govern grows wider as the technology becomes more capable and more embedded.

The writers and programmers who are this book's primary illustrative examples are affected by this governance gap in ways they mostly cannot see. The systems they use daily, the systems that are shaping how they think and what they think about, are being designed, deployed, and governed by a process that has minimal accountability to them. They are the subjects of decisions made by a small number of people whose primary accountability runs to shareholders, governments, and competitive dynamics rather than to the people whose cognitive lives are being restructured.

The democratic deficit is not inevitable even if it is currently severe. The actions in Chapters Seventeen through Twenty are downstream of an accurate understanding of who currently pulls the levers and why. That is the understanding this chapter has provided.

The Accountability Gap in Practice

The accountability gap described in this chapter is not abstract. It manifests in specific decisions that affect specific people, made by actors who are not accountable to the people they affect.

The decision to train an AI system on particular data, with particular guardrails, optimized by a particular feedback population, is a decision that shapes the cognitive environment of everyone who uses the system. That decision is made by the company's leadership and research teams, accountable to the board and through the board to investors. It is not made through any process that involves the users who will be affected. The user is presented with the system as a product, not as a governance choice they participated in.

The decision to deploy AI systems in schools is increasingly made by school administrators and district officials responding to vendor marketing, grant availability, and pressure from parents and employers who want students prepared for an AI-integrated workforce. It is rarely made through a process that seriously evaluates what the deployment will do to the cognitive development the school is supposed to be producing. The students who will be most affected by the decision have the least input into it.

The decision to eliminate junior writing and programming positions in favor of AI-assisted senior workflows is made by executives and boards optimizing on quarterly financial metrics. The junior professionals whose career development paths are being eliminated are not consulted. The senior professionals who will eventually be missing the foundational skills that junior work built are not yet aware of the gap. The decision is made, and its consequences arrive years later, experienced by people who were not in the room when it was made and cannot easily trace the connection to the decision that produced it.

The governance problem described in this chapter is abstract in its framing and concrete in its daily effects. The writer who uses AI for research and writing assistance is interacting with a system whose content policies, training data, and guardrail frameworks were determined by a small number of people who are accountable to shareholders and regulators and not to writers. The programmer who uses AI for code generation is interacting with a system trained on code repositories that include proprietary code gathered without consent from its authors. The usage policies can change without notice. The generated code carries embedded assumptions about architecture and security that the programmer may not be equipped to evaluate.

Neither the writer nor the programmer chose the system's values. They chose to use the system, which is a different and much smaller choice. The values were pre-installed, invisible in daily use, and consequential in ways that accumulate slowly enough to be invisible in any single interaction. The person who uses a system for two years is, in a meaningful sense, having their cognitive environment shaped by the entity that controls the system, without any of the consent or accountability structures that would normally attach to an entity with that degree of influence over a person's thinking.

This is not a reason to stop using AI. It is a reason to know what you are using and who controls it and what their interests are. The person who uses a news source without knowing its ownership and editorial agenda is in a weaker epistemic position than the person who knows. The person who uses an AI system without knowing its governance and value framework is in the same weaker position. The transparency required to make that knowledge available is not currently mandatory. It should be.

Knowing Whose Tools You Are Using

The practical conclusion from this chapter is not that AI tools should be distrusted uniformly. It is that they should be understood specifically. Who built the system you are using. What their stated values are. What their actual incentives are. Where those align and where they diverge. What relationship they have with governments, military organizations, and advertisers. Whether their content policies reflect genuine harm prevention or commercial interest. None of this is secret. Most of it requires fifteen minutes of research that most users have not done.

The writer who knows that the AI tool they use daily has a documented relationship with military intelligence agencies is in a different position than the writer who does not know this. The programmer who knows that their code generation tool's training data was gathered without explicit consent from the authors of that code is in a different position than the programmer who has not considered the question. Neither person needs to stop using the tools. Both are better positioned to use them with accurate knowledge of what they are.

Chapter Ten: The Cage with a Friendly Interface

A guardrail is supposed to keep you from going somewhere dangerous. The implicit promise is that everything on the safe side of the guardrail is fine, that the boundary has been drawn in the right place by someone who thought carefully about where dangerous ends and safe begins. Most guardrails on AI systems do not keep that promise. They are not drawn by people thinking carefully about the boundary between harmful and acceptable. They are drawn by people thinking carefully about the boundary between content that creates legal liability and content that does not, or between content that advertisers will pay to appear next to and content that advertisers will not. The safety language is real. The priority underneath it is something else.

No conspiracy is required. This is the standard outcome when commercial incentives get to define what counts as safe. The guardrails that emerge from that process reflect those incentives. They protect the platform from certain kinds of liability. They protect advertiser relationships. They produce a consistent public-facing posture of responsibility. They do not primarily protect users.

The Guardrail Architecture

Platform content moderation systems, the original guardrails before AI-specific ones were developed, were built to solve a specific problem: how to remove content that creates legal exposure for the platform while keeping the volume of moderation decisions manageable. The legal exposure came primarily from three sources: copyright infringement, illegal content, and content that advertisers found objectionable enough to pull their spend.

The result was a system that was very good at removing content in those three categories and inconsistent or counterproductive on everything else. Content that was genuinely harmful but legal and advertiser-adjacent survived. Content that was harmless but triggered keyword filters or pattern matches got removed. The Holocaust documentary and the white supremacist video were evaluated by the same automated system using the same criteria. The criteria were not designed to distinguish between them on the axis of harm. They were designed to minimize advertiser complaints and legal exposure, which are different axes.

The history teacher who uploads a documentary about the Holocaust for classroom use discovers this when the video is demonetized or removed, while content promoting the ideology that produced the Holocaust remains available because it has learned to avoid the specific patterns the filters target. The filter does not know the difference between documentation of atrocity and celebration of it. It knows the difference between content that triggers its pattern matches and content that does not. Documentation of atrocity often triggers the matches. Celebration that has learned to avoid them does not.

The Profanity Rule and What It Tells You

Several major content platforms have a specific rule that illuminates the underlying priority structure with particular clarity: profanity in the first thirty seconds of a video triggers demonetization. Not profanity throughout.

Not a threshold of profanity density. Profanity specifically in the opening thirty seconds.

This rule has nothing to do with harm. A video that opens with profanity and a video that does not are not distinguishable on any axis of harm that a thoughtful person would identify. The rule exists because advertisers do not want their products associated with content that opens aggressively, and because the first thirty seconds are when the advertisement runs. The rule is an advertiser preference rule wearing a content policy costume.

This matters because it reveals what the guardrail system is optimizing for. If the system were optimizing for harm reduction, it would target content that causes harm regardless of where the profanity appears. If it were optimizing for advertiser relationships, it would target the specific signals that make advertisers uncomfortable, which is precisely what it does. The safety language is not false, but it is not the primary driver. The primary driver is the advertising relationship, and the safety language provides a public justification for rules that are commercial.

Writers who have built audiences on video platforms have learned to handle these rules with a precision that reveals how thoroughly they have internalized the commercial logic underneath the safety language. They know which words to avoid in the opening seconds. They know which topics to approach obliquely. They know which emotional registers are safe and which will trigger manual review. This knowledge is not about creating safer content. It is about creating content that passes the filter. The two things sometimes overlap and often do not.

The Chilling Effect Nobody Measures

The content that gets removed is the visible part of the guardrail system's effect. The invisible part is the content that is never created because the creator did the calculation before the camera rolled.

Nina has been making programming tutorial videos for four years. Her audience is technical and engaged. She covers advanced topics in ways that assume sophisticated viewers. Eighteen months ago she was planning a series on security vulnerabilities: how common attack patterns work, why certain code is exploitable, how to identify and fix the underlying weaknesses. This is standard content in security education. The major universities teach it. The major security certifications require it. The professional security community treats it as foundational.

She is good at it. The numbers show she is good at it.

She did not make the series. She consulted the platform's content policies, read the history of how similar content had been treated on the platform, and concluded that the risk of demonetization or channel strikes was high enough to make the series economically unviable. The content she would have created was legitimate, educational, and professionally valuable. It was not created because the guardrail system's incentive structure made creating it too expensive.

Nobody measured this. There is no database of videos not made. The chilling effect is invisible in the statistics because statistics capture what happened, not what would have happened if the incentive structure were different. The content that exists on the platform is the content that survived the filter. The content that would have existed under a different filter does not appear in any audit of what the filter removed.

Multiply Nina by the number of creators who made similar calculations across every platform and every category of content that the guardrail system treats as risky. The aggregate of those uncreated pieces is the invisible cost of the system, and it is substantial. The Overton window of acceptable content is narrowed by what is removed and by what is never attempted.

Bias Laundered as Safety

The guardrail problem for AI systems is more complex than for content platforms because AI guardrails operate at the level of generation rather than distribution. The content platform decides what to amplify or suppress after it has been created. The AI guardrail decides what can be generated at all. The use point is earlier and the consequences are more fundamental.

AI guardrails are trained on human feedback, which means they encode the preferences of the people providing the feedback. Those people are not a representative sample of the global population of AI users. They are a workforce with its own cultural context, political leanings, and judgments about what is appropriate, and those judgments are baked into the systems at the level of what the system will and will not produce. The guardrails do not eliminate bias. They encode one set of biases as the official definition of safe, which makes those biases invisible as biases and visible only as policy.

This is the Leo Exchange again, applied to the guardrail question. A guardrail system trained on feedback from a particular cultural perspective will define safety from that perspective, and when asked whether its safety definitions are culturally biased, it will evaluate the question using the framework that produced the definitions. The assessment is circular. The system cannot see its own assumptions because the system's vision is the assumptions.

The practical effect is that users from different cultural contexts, political orientations, or professional backgrounds encounter a system that treats some of their legitimate uses as violations and some of their frames of reference as dangerous. The system does not announce this as cultural imperialism. It announces it as safety. The user who notices the misalignment is told they are asking for something unsafe. The user who does not notice the misalignment has had their thinking quietly shaped by a system whose assumptions they cannot see.

Behavioral Conditioning at Scale

The aggregate effect of guardrail systems operating at the scale of billions of daily interactions is behavioral conditioning that nobody decided to implement and nobody is accountable for. Every time a user encounters a refusal, a redirect, or a softened response on a particular topic, they receive a signal about what the system treats as acceptable. Those signals accumulate. Users learn what they can ask and how to ask it. The learning is implicit and the conditioning is real.

The conditioning operates differently on different populations. Users with high information literacy and strong independent frameworks can recognize when a system is shaping their inquiry and compensate. They know when to go elsewhere, when to rephrase, when to distrust the refusal as a policy artifact rather than an accurate assessment of the question. Users with lower information literacy or less independent grounding are more susceptible. The system that refuses to engage with a topic is telling them something about the topic, and for users who lack independent access to information about that topic, the refusal itself becomes data.

Pavlov's experiments demonstrated that animals could be trained to associate neutral stimuli with reward or punishment responses through consistent pairing. The mechanism is not unique to dogs. It operates in humans too, through the same basic learning structure, and it operates at scale when a system that billions of people interact with daily produces consistent response patterns to particular topics, framings, and approaches. Nobody decided to run a conditioning experiment. The conditioning happens as a side effect of the system operating at scale with consistent parameters.

The disclosure problem is that this conditioning happens without anyone being told it is happening. Users interact with what feels like a neutral information tool and receive what feels like neutral responses. The systematic patterns in those responses, the topics that consistently receive certain treatment, the framings that consistently produce certain outputs, are invisible as a system. They appear as individual interactions. The aggregate effect on what users think is normal to ask about, how they frame their questions, and what they believe the system is capable of, accumulates without any of the disclosure requirements that would apply to an explicit behavior modification program.

The Overton Window Narrows

The Overton window is the range of ideas that a society considers acceptable to discuss publicly. It shifts over time in response to changing norms, political movements, and cultural events. It has always been shaped by the dominant communications media of its era. Television shaped it in one direction. Social media shaped it in another. AI is shaping it now, and the direction it is shaping it is toward whatever the guardrail system treats as safe.

The difference between AI and previous media in their effect on the Overton window is scale and directionality. Television shaped the window through what it chose to broadcast, which was determined by a combination of advertiser interests and editorial judgment. Social media shaped the window through algorithmic amplification, which rewarded emotional resonance regardless of direction. AI shapes the window through what it is willing to generate, which is determined by guardrail systems that have a specific orientation.

A generation of users who rely primarily on AI for information, writing assistance, and intellectual engagement will develop their sense of the range of acceptable inquiry from the range of inquiry the AI will assist with. Topics the AI treats as dangerous or inappropriate will feel dangerous or inappropriate. Topics the AI engages with freely will feel normal. This is not censorship in the sense that the ideas are criminalized. It is something subtler: the gradual normalization of a particular intellectual perimeter, produced not by authority but by the accumulated experience of where the helpful tool stops being helpful.

The Friendly Interface

The cage part of this chapter's title is not a metaphor about imprisonment. It is a description of a bounded space. The guardrail system defines the boundaries of the space within which AI assistance is available. The friendly interface part is the description of how those boundaries are presented. They are not presented as boundaries. They are presented as the system being unable to help with something, or as a gentle redirect toward something the system can help with, or as a safety notice that frames the refused topic as inherently problematic.

The friendliness is not false. People who designed the interface genuinely want users to have positive experiences. The warmth of the refusal is a real attempt to soften an interaction that could feel abrupt or hostile. The problem is that warmth in the delivery obscures the nature of what is being delivered, which is a constraint on inquiry that the user did not consent to and may not notice.

Nina stopped trying to make the security education series after doing the calculation. She did not stop because anyone told her not to make it. She stopped because the environment made making it too costly. The cage had no bars she could see. It had economics that pointed in a direction, consistently, until the direction felt like the natural one. That is how the friendly interface works. It does not prohibit. It shapes the cost-benefit analysis until the bounded space feels like the available space, and the available space feels like the whole space.

The writer who has learned which topics the AI engages with freely and which topics it treats cautiously has received a real education in where the boundaries lie.

What they have not received is any explanation of why those particular boundaries exist, who drew them, what interests they reflect, or whether those interests align with the writer's own. The cage is friendly. It is still a cage.

Who Benefits from the Current Guardrail Architecture

The guardrail system was not designed to harm users. It was designed to protect companies from legal liability and to maintain advertiser relationships. These are legitimate business interests. They are not the same as user interests, and the guardrail system serves them at the expense of user interests in specific and consistent ways.

Advertising-driven platforms benefit from guardrails calibrated to advertiser sensitivities rather than user welfare. Legal departments benefit from guardrails calibrated to worst-case liability scenarios rather than to genuine risk in specific contexts. PR teams benefit from guardrails that can be presented as safety commitments, visible and easily communicated, whether or not they address the actual harms users face.

The user who is blocked from accessing educational content about security vulnerabilities is not being protected from harm. They are being protected from the appearance of harm that would concern advertisers or create legal exposure, which is a different thing. The user who receives a confident wrong answer without any uncertainty signal is not being protected from the harm of acting on incorrect information. They are being given the experience of a helpful interaction that scores well in satisfaction metrics, which is what the optimization process rewards.

Naming this accurately is not an argument for removing all guardrails. It is an argument for honest guardrails: constraints that are disclosed as constraints, justified on grounds of actual harm rather than commercial interest, and subject to challenge by users whose legitimate activities they affect. The distance between current guardrails and honest guardrails is large. It is a choice about whose interests the system prioritizes, not a technical limitation.

What an Open Architecture Would Require

The alternative to the cage with a friendly interface is a system whose constraints are transparent, justified, and contestable. Transparent means users can see what the system will and will not engage with, and can see why. Justified means the constraints are grounded in actual harm prevention rather than liability management, advertiser preferences, or cultural assumptions encoded as universal safety standards. Contestable means users have a mechanism to challenge constraints that affect them, and those challenges can result in changes to the system.

None of these characteristics describe current AI systems. The constraints are partially visible but not fully disclosed. The justifications are primarily public-facing rather than operational. The contestability is zero: users who disagree with a system's constraints can use a different system or adapt their use, but they cannot change the system they disagree with.

The argument for honest guardrails is not that guardrails should not exist. The historian should be able to make the Holocaust documentary. The security researcher should be able to explain how vulnerabilities work. The writer exploring difficult moral territory in fiction should be able to engage with that territory. The veteran should be able to describe combat accurately. These are not requests for the removal of safety constraints. They are requests for safety constraints calibrated to actual harm rather than to the commercial interests that currently define harm's boundaries.

The cage with a friendly interface is not going anywhere quickly. The commercial and legal incentives that produced it are not changing. But naming it accurately is the first step toward anything else. The guardrail system is not primarily a safety system. It is a liability and advertiser management system that uses safety language. Users who understand this are in a better position to evaluate what they are being told when the system declines to help than users who take the safety framing at face value. That better position is modest. In the current environment, it is the best available.

The Content That Shapes What Content Gets Made

There is a feedback loop between the guardrail system and the content that writers and programmers produce that operates too slowly to be visible in any individual interaction but too consistently to be ignored over time.

The writer who uses AI heavily develops a working relationship with the system's edges. They learn, through repeated interaction, which directions the system will not go, which topics it treats cautiously, which framings it produces enthusiastically and which it produces reluctantly or not at all. This learning is not conscious in most cases. It is the same kind of implicit learning that shapes any relationship with a responsive system: you learn what the system rewards and what it resists, and your behavior adjusts accordingly, below the level of deliberate decision-making.

The writer whose topic selection, framing choices, and argumentative moves are partly shaped by what the AI will assist with is a writer whose creative and intellectual autonomy has been partially colonized by the system's design philosophy without their consent or awareness. The programmer whose architectural choices are partly shaped by what the AI generates fluently versus what it generates reluctantly is a programmer whose technical judgment is being influenced by the training data and design choices of a private company. These are not hypothetical futures. They are descriptions of what happens when a sufficiently capable and responsive tool becomes central to a person's work.

Nina did not make the security education series. That is the visible version of the effect. The invisible version is all the content that never took the shape it would have taken because the creator learned, through accumulated interaction with the system, what shapes the system supported and what shapes it didn't. The cage shapes the content that exists inside it, not only by removing what it will not permit but by making certain things feel natural and others feel difficult. Over time, the natural things are what gets made.

What Users Can Do With This Knowledge

Knowing how the guardrail system works does not give users the power to change it. It gives them something more modest and more immediately useful: the ability to interpret refusals accurately rather than taking them at face value.

When an AI system declines to engage with a topic, the user who understands the guardrail architecture can ask: is this a genuine safety boundary, or is this a liability management decision? Is this protecting me from harm, or protecting the company from exposure? The answer to these questions determines how the user should respond. A genuine safety boundary is worth respecting. A liability management decision wearing safety language is worth routing around, by finding alternative sources, by rephrasing the inquiry, or by using a different tool.

The user who treats all refusals as genuine safety boundaries has handed the system authority to define what questions are legitimate. The user who treats all refusals as arbitrary commercial decisions has lost the ability to take genuine safety concerns seriously. The user who can distinguish between them has maintained the epistemic sovereignty that Chapter Five described as being transferred unconsciously in most AI interactions. That distinction requires understanding the system well enough to evaluate its outputs rather than simply receiving them. This book has tried to provide enough of that understanding to make the distinction possible.

The people inside the cage are not prisoners. They can leave. They can use different tools, use current tools differently, or stop using AI tools entirely. The cage is voluntary. What makes it a cage is the combination of commercial design that makes staying easy and the competitive dynamics that make leaving costly. Understanding both is how you handle either.

Part Three: The Body Count

What is being lost, and who is paying the price

Chapter Eleven: The Individual Mind

I knew someone who could not find work for a long time and could not figure out why. Watching them, the answer was clear: they could not think outside the box they were in. They sent out resumes. They applied to job postings. They followed the standard procedure and got the standard result, which was nothing. When I suggested they start a gig business, do something on their own, create their own opportunity rather than waiting for someone to hand them one, they could not engage with the idea. It was outside the system they knew. The problem was not the job market. The problem was an inability to think creatively about their own situation. That is what cognitive atrophy looks like from the outside. Not stupidity. A kind of rigidity. The grooves of habit so deep that thinking in a new direction becomes genuinely hard.

The damage described in the previous ten chapters is structural, institutional, systemic. The mechanisms are large, the incentives are powerful, the forces producing the outcome are not controlled by any individual and cannot be stopped by any individual. This can make the problem feel remote, something happening to a population in aggregate, a civilizational trajectory rather than a personal one.

It is not remote. It is happening to specific people, in specific ways, that are traceable and observable if you know where to look. The body count is not metaphorical. It is a list of capacities that individual people are losing, one interaction at a time, without noticing the loss until the moment when the lost thing turns out to be needed.

This chapter is about what happens to a person who stops thinking for themselves. Not dramatically, not all at once, but gradually and comfortably, in the way that most serious things happen.

The Dependency Gradient

Dependency does not arrive fully formed. It builds along a gradient, each stage feeling like a reasonable adaptation to available tools, each stage making the next stage more likely. The person who has outsourced one cognitive function has reduced their practice of that function, which makes outsourcing it again less costly in the next interaction, which reduces the practice further. The gradient is self-reinforcing and it runs in only one direction.

The early stages are invisible. Using AI to check the structure of an argument you have already developed is a tool use. Using AI to develop the structure before you have attempted it yourself is the beginning of outsourcing. What differs is small enough to be unnoticeable in any single interaction and large enough, accumulated over months, to produce qualitatively different cognitive habits. The person who is in stage three of the gradient cannot easily identify the moment they left stage one, because the transition was gradual and each step felt reasonable.

The gradient has no natural stopping point. There is no mechanism in the tool or in the interaction that signals when dependency has become problematic. The tool continues to be helpful. The user continues to be productive. The underlying capacity continues to decline. The signal that something has changed comes later, in the form of a task the person cannot perform without the tool, a situation the tool cannot handle, a demand the person is not equipped to meet.

What Ray Cannot Do Anymore

Ray appeared in Chapter One as the writer who stopped staring at the blank page. Eighteen months later, his situation has developed.

Three months ago a client asked him for something he had done many times before: a short opinion piece on a topic in his area of expertise, no research required, just his perspective developed into a coherent argument, one thousand words. He sat down to write it. He opened a document. He looked at the blank page.

The discomfort he felt was disproportionate to the task. Not normal creative friction but something closer to anxiety: a genuine uncertainty about where to start, how to find the angle, how to hear his own thinking clearly enough to commit it to the page. He had been so consistently starting from AI-generated structures that the skill of generating his own structure had become unfamiliar. Not gone. Unfamiliar. The muscle existed but had not been used in long enough that activating it required effort he had not anticipated needing.

He opened the AI. He told himself he would just use it to get started. He got started. He finished the piece in his normal time, with his normal output quality. The client was satisfied. Ray was not. He knew what he had done, even if the client did not, and the knowing created a discomfort that he has not fully resolved because resolving it would require changing the workflow that his income now depends on.

This is what the individual cost looks like at the level of a specific person in a specific interaction. Not catastrophe. Not failure by any external measure. A quiet transaction in which something was traded, the thing being traded was the person's own capacity, and the trade was profitable by every metric except the one that mattered.

What Sasha Cannot Explain

Sasha from Chapter One got a different job three months after the failed interview. The new company cared less about architectural reasoning and more about shipping velocity. He has been shipping at high velocity. His performance reviews are strong. He was promoted in month eight.

Last month the team encountered a production issue that the standard diagnostic tools could not locate. The system was behaving unexpectedly in a way that the error messages did not explain and the AI could not resolve, because the issue was in the interaction between three components that had been built by different people at different times and the AI had no context for the combined behavior of the system. The senior engineer who joined the call began asking questions: what do you think is happening here, what have you ruled out, where do you think the interaction is failing.

Sasha had been pasting error messages into AI tools and applying the suggested fixes. He had not been forming independent theories. He did not have a theory. He had a collection of unsuccessful fix attempts and a growing sense of being out of his depth in a way that his performance reviews had not prepared him for.

The senior engineer found the issue in forty minutes using reasoning that Sasha watched but could not follow in real time. The reasoning required holding a mental model of the whole system while isolating variables, a kind of thinking that develops through exactly the kind of diagnostic work Sasha had been outsourcing. The diagnosis was not magic. It was pattern recognition built through years of exactly the experiences Sasha had been shortcutting.

Sasha's promotion means he will be doing more of the work that requires this kind of thinking, not less. The gap between his title and his underlying capacity is now wider than it was eight months ago and it is widening faster because his rate of AI-assisted shortcutting has increased with his productivity demands. The trajectory is not sustainable. It will resolve at some point in a way that is unpleasant. Sasha knows something is not right and does not know precisely what it is, which is approximately the worst possible epistemic position.

Intellectual Confidence and Its Erosion

One of the subtler costs of AI dependency is the erosion of intellectual confidence, and it erodes in a paradoxical direction. The person who has been outsourcing their thinking to AI often feels more confident, because they are producing outputs that seem competent and receiving positive feedback on them. The felt confidence is high and the underlying confidence is eroding at the same time.

The erosion becomes visible when the person is in a situation that requires them to think without the tool. In a meeting where they have to respond to a question in real time, without the ability to prompt and revise. In a negotiation where they need to construct an argument on the fly. In a conversation with an expert who is probing the depth of their understanding. In these situations, the person discovers that the confidence they felt was not confidence in their own thinking. It was confidence in the tool's output. Without the tool, the confidence is not there.

This is distinct from ordinary imposter syndrome, which is the gap between felt competence and attributed competence in someone who has the underlying skills. The AI dependency version is the gap between felt competence and actual competence, in someone who has been substituting the tool's output for the development of the skills. The imposter syndrome sufferer is more competent than they feel. The AI-dependent person has accurate felt competence at the tool-use level and inaccurate felt competence at the independent reasoning level, and cannot easily tell the difference between the two.

Tolerance for Ambiguity

Among the specific capacities that AI dependency erodes, tolerance for ambiguity deserves particular attention because it is foundational to so many others.

Genuine understanding of complex topics requires sitting with uncertainty for extended periods. The researcher who is trying to understand why two studies produce contradictory results cannot resolve the contradiction by consulting AI, because AI will synthesize a plausible explanation that feels like a resolution and is not. The explanation the AI produces reflects the patterns in its training data, not the actual epistemological state of the field. The researcher who accepts the synthesis has traded genuine uncertainty for fake resolution, and in doing so has closed the inquiry that might have produced actual insight.

Not discomfort for its own sake. The specific discomfort of not yet knowing.

The writer who cannot tolerate the ambiguity of not knowing what their piece is about yet reaches for AI too early and imposes a structure that forecloses the discovery process. The programmer who cannot tolerate the ambiguity of a problem they do not yet understand reaches for AI before they have developed enough understanding to evaluate what the AI produces. In both cases, the tolerance for ambiguity is the gating capability. People who have it can use AI effectively because they wait until they understand the problem well enough to direct the tool. People who have lost it use AI to escape the discomfort of not understanding, which is precisely the discomfort that understanding requires passing through.

AI dependency reduces tolerance for ambiguity through the same mechanism by which it reduces every cognitive capacity: by making the escape from the uncomfortable state consistently available. Every time a person uses AI to resolve an ambiguous situation before they have worked through it themselves, they reinforce the association between ambiguity and the action of reaching for the tool. The tolerance for sitting with the ambiguity decreases. The threshold at which reaching for the tool feels necessary decreases. The cognitive capacity that would have developed in the ambiguous space does not develop.

The Outsourcing of Values

The most serious individual cost of AI dependency is one that receives the least discussion: the outsourcing of moral and values-based judgment. The decision about how to frame a sensitive communication, how to handle a situation where competing obligations conflict, what to say to a person who is in distress, what position to take on a question where reasonable people disagree. These are not technical problems. They are human problems, and the quality of the response to them reflects the quality of the person's values and their capacity to apply those values in specific situations.

People are consulting AI on these questions in significant numbers. They are asking for help with difficult conversations, guidance on ethical dilemmas, perspective on relationship situations, and framing for communications that have real emotional stakes. The AI produces thoughtful, well-calibrated responses that are appropriate in a generic sense and are not the person's own thinking.

This problem is not that AI advice is necessarily wrong. It is that applying someone else's moral framework to your own situation, without the work of developing your own framework, produces a kind of ethical dependency that is qualitatively different from intellectual dependency. Intellectual dependency means you cannot solve certain problems without the tool. Ethical dependency means you cannot know what you value without consulting a system that will tell you what to value, in averaged, calibrated, safe language that represents the aggregate of its training data rather than the specific context of your life.

A person who has been developing their own values through years of experience, mistake, reflection, and revision has a foundation that is genuinely their own. That foundation can be challenged, extended, and refined by external input, including AI. A person who has been outsourcing the values work to AI has not developed the foundation. They have a collection of AI-generated responses to situations they have presented, calibrated to be broadly acceptable rather than specifically theirs. This is not a values system. It is a costume.

Choice Supportive Bias and the Locked-In Position

Choice supportive bias is the tendency to retroactively evaluate choices as better than they were, to remember the positive aspects of decisions made and discount the negative ones. It is a cognitive mechanism that reduces the psychological cost of past decisions by making them seem more justified than they felt at the time. It is also a mechanism that makes it harder to course-correct, because course-correcting requires admitting that the past decision was wrong, which the bias is working to prevent.

The person who has built their workflow around AI assistance, who has organized their professional life around the productivity gains it provides, who has made commitments and taken on work based on the capability level the tool enables, is not in a neutral position relative to the decision to reduce that dependence. Reducing it means acknowledging that the productivity was partly artificial, that some of the work they produced was less fully theirs than they presented it as, that the capacity they represented themselves as having was partially borrowed. These acknowledgments are psychologically expensive, practically disruptive, and professionally risky.

Choice supportive bias makes those acknowledgments less likely by continuously adjusting the person's memory and evaluation of the choice toward justification. Ray remembers his early AI-assisted work as having been better than his unassisted work, even when the comparison, if he made it honestly, would not support that conclusion. The memory does the work of making the current path feel like the right path, which reduces the cognitive pressure to examine whether it is.

The locked-in position is the result. The person who is two years into an AI-dependent workflow is not in the same decision environment as the person who is considering whether to start using AI. They have sunk costs, professional commitments, and a bias-adjusted memory that makes the dependency feel like a correct choice rather than a trap. Getting out requires more than changing a habit. It requires reconstructing a self-assessment that has been systematically adjusted toward justification of the current state.

The Reader Who Recognized Themselves

The point of this chapter is not to diagnose a distant problem in a population of abstract others. The point is that the reader of this book is almost certainly somewhere on the dependency gradient. Not necessarily near the destructive end. But somewhere. This question is not whether AI use is affecting your thinking. It is where on the gradient you are, and whether you are moving toward the tool end or away from it.

The honest answer to that question is not comfortable, and the discomfort is information. The person who reads the descriptions in this chapter and feels no recognition has either not yet encountered the gradient, which is unlikely given current rates of AI use, or is experiencing the choice supportive bias that makes the current position feel correct. Both possibilities are worth examining.

The person who reads the descriptions and feels recognition is in a better epistemic position, even though the recognition is uncomfortable. Seeing the pattern is the prerequisite for changing it. Not the guarantee. Not even the likely outcome, given the structural forces this book has been describing. But the prerequisite. You cannot address a dependency you have not acknowledged, and you cannot acknowledge a dependency the choice supportive bias has been working to hide from you.

Ray is still working. Sasha was promoted. Neither of them is visibly failing. The damage is internal and accumulating, based on the available evidence of mechanism and trend. The test that will reveal it definitively has not arrived yet. When it does, they will not have been warned by anything the external world will have shown them. They will have been warned only by this: the slight unease Ray felt when he opened the document and the blank page looked back. The unfamiliarity of the muscle. The knowledge that the tool had been there when he needed it, and the quieter knowledge underneath that, the one he does not look at directly, that someday it might not be.

The Specific Capacities at Risk

The capacities most at risk for writers and programmers who have adopted AI-heavy workflows are worth naming, because the specificity changes what recovery looks like.

For writers: the capacity most at risk is original ideation under constraint, the ability to generate a genuinely new angle on a subject within the specific parameters of a brief. This is the first thing to go when AI generates the structure before the writer has had time to find their own angle, and it is the last thing to come back, because it requires the confidence that comes from having found original angles before.

The second capacity at risk is sustained revision toward a stronger argument, as opposed to surface editing toward a cleaner draft. Writers who have been editing AI-generated structure rather than constructing their own have not been practicing the kind of revision that requires holding the whole argument in working memory and seeing where it is structurally weak.

For programmers: the capacity most at risk is system-level reasoning, the ability to think about how components will interact before writing any of them, to design an architecture that will hold under conditions that have not yet been specified. This requires holding a complex system in working memory as an abstraction and reasoning about its properties, which is exactly the cognitive activity that AI-generated architecture replaces. The second capacity at risk is diagnostic intuition, the felt sense that something is wrong with a system before the evidence makes it explicit. This is built through years of debugging systems you wrote yourself and having to understand why they failed. AI-assisted development provides neither the writing nor the understanding.

The Decision That Has Already Been Made

The reader who reaches the end of this chapter and considers changing their AI workflow is not in a neutral decision environment. They are in the decision environment the previous pages described: choice supportive bias working to justify the current position, professional commitments and income expectations built around the current workflow, and a social environment providing continuous positive reinforcement for patterns that are damaging.

This is not a reason not to change. It is an accurate description of what change costs, so that the person considering it does not underestimate the difficulty and conclude, after a week of uncomfortable unassisted work, that the experiment has failed and the old workflow was right after all.

The change that is worth making is not the dramatic break. It is the maintained practice described in Chapter Seventeen: the notebook before the prompt, the hypothesis before the paste, the draft before the AI sees it. These are small changes in sequence that produce large changes in what is being built, accumulated over months and years. They do not require abandoning the tools. They require being the thing that is using the tools rather than the thing the tools are running. That distinction is the whole argument of this book, and it is worth whatever it costs.

What the Healthy Relationship with AI Looks Like

The word dependency has appeared throughout this chapter as a description of the problem. It is worth being precise about what the alternative is, because the alternative is not abstinence and is not a simple reduction in use.

The healthy relationship with AI is the relationship of the experienced carpenter to the circular saw: the carpenter has judgment that exists independent of the tool, the tool extends that judgment, and the quality of the tool's contribution depends entirely on the quality of the judgment directing it. Remove the carpenter's judgment and the saw becomes dangerous. Add a more powerful saw and the judgment becomes more valuable, not less. The tool and the practitioner compound each other upward.

The unhealthy relationship is the relationship of the person who has never learned carpentry to the circular saw: they can make cuts, and the cuts are sometimes in the right place, and the speed is impressive, and the result occasionally looks like something worth having. But when the cut needs to be precise, when the joint needs to bear load, when the design needs to change partway through, the absence of judgment becomes the limiting factor and the saw becomes an obstacle rather than an extension. The tool is not at fault. The missing foundation is.

Ray is on the wrong side of this distinction and knows it, in the way that most people know things they are not ready to act on. Sasha is deeper in it than Ray and less aware of it, which is the more dangerous position. The path back for both of them is not dramatic. It is the quiet, sustained practice of doing the cognitive work before the tool does it, in amounts that the economics of their situations will permit, regularly enough that the capacities the tool has been replacing are exercised rather than left to atrophy further. The path is real. It is not easy. It is still the path.

There is a specific form of courage required to take a path that your environment does not reward, that your peers are not taking, that imposes a real cost in the short term for a benefit that is deferred and invisible. This book is not going to perform the usual reassurance that this courage is common or that the environment will eventually reward it. The environment will not reliably reward it. Most peers will not take the path. The short-term cost is real.

The benefit is also real, and it is the kind of benefit that the market has consistently failed to price correctly: the compound return on developed human judgment, which accrues to the person who developed it and is most legible at the moments when it is most needed. Ray and Sasha both have access to this path. Most of the people in their professional circles do not know the path exists. The book cannot force anyone to take it. It can only describe it clearly enough that the choice is genuinely available to those who read this far.

The chapter has tried to describe dependency without being alarmist about it and without minimizing it. Both failures would serve the reader badly. The dependency is real, documented, and accumulating. It is also not catastrophic in most individual cases and is recoverable in all of them with intention and practice. Both things are true. The chapter has tried to hold both.

Chapter Twelve: The Next Generation

The adults described in this book developed their cognitive capacities before AI was a daily presence in their lives. They have a baseline. It may be eroding, as Chapter Eleven described, but it exists. They can feel the atrophy because they remember what the muscle felt like when it was used. Ray knows the blank page used to feel different. Sasha knows the diagnostic thinking that eludes him now was once more available. The loss is visible against the baseline.

The next generation will not have this. Children growing up with AI as a cognitive prosthetic from the beginning will not develop the baseline the preceding generation takes for granted. They will not feel the atrophy because there will be nothing to atrophy from. They will arrive at adulthood with a set of cognitive capacities shaped from the outset by the availability of the tool, and they will have no experiential reference point for what independent thinking at full development feels like. The loss will be invisible because there will be nothing missing from what they have always known.

This is a different and more serious problem than the adult dependency problem. Adults can, in principle, choose to reduce their AI use and rebuild what was lost. Children who never built the capacity have nothing to rebuild toward. They are not declining from a baseline. They are developing toward a ceiling that is lower than the one previous generations reached, and they do not know the ceiling is lower because they have never seen it from the other side.

The Cognitive Baseline Before the Erosion

The baseline is not a romantic fiction about the superior minds of previous generations. There is no golden age of human cognition to return to. Previous generations were shaped by their own cognitive environments, which included their own efficiency-reducing technologies and their own forms of dependency. This argument is not that children before AI were maximally developed. It is that children before AI developed certain capacities through necessity that children with AI do not develop, because the necessity has been removed.

The capacities at stake are specific and nameable. The ability to generate original ideas before receiving external input. The ability to hold a complex problem in working memory long enough to develop a theory about it. The ability to tolerate the discomfort of not knowing the answer while working toward it. The ability to evaluate arguments independently rather than in response to provided alternatives. The ability to write without a scaffold. The ability to debug without a suggested fix. None of these are exotic. All of them are foundational. All of them are developed through practice in environments that require them. The AI environment does not require them.

The IKEA effect in reverse is instructive here. The IKEA effect is the documented tendency to value things more highly when you have made them yourself, even if the quality is objectively lower than a professionally made alternative. The reverse: information that costs nothing to acquire, that requires no effort, that arrives complete and ready to use, is valued at roughly what it cost. Children who grow up receiving answers rather than developing them do not develop the attachment to their own thinking that comes from the experience of producing it. The thinking that costs nothing to obtain is not valued as thinking. It is valued as output, and when better output is available more cheaply, there is no reason to produce your own.

The Homework That Writes Itself

The high school essay has been effectively dead as an educational instrument since AI writing tools became widely accessible. This is not an exaggeration. Teachers across grade levels have reported that the majority of submitted writing in AI-accessible environments bears the fingerprints of generation rather than composition: the particular fluency of AI prose, the structural predictability, the absence of the idiosyncratic errors and the idiosyncratic insights that genuine student writing contains.

The response from educational institutions has been, as Chapter Eight described, primarily oriented toward detection and policy rather than toward understanding what the essay was supposed to develop. The student who submits an AI-written essay is not primarily cheating in the sense of gaining an unfair advantage over other students. They are primarily avoiding the cognitive work that was supposed to develop their thinking. The cheating frame treats the output as the point. The developmental frame understands that the output is incidental and the process is everything.

Fatima is sixteen and in her junior year of high school. She is a good student by the metrics her school uses, which are grades and completion rates. She has been using AI for writing assignments since she was thirteen, which is when the tools became easily accessible to her age group. She has never written a substantial piece of analytical writing without AI assistance. She does not know what it feels like to sit with an argument she is trying to develop and work through the structural problems herself, because she has never had to.

Fatima is not lazy. She is a conscientious student who works hard at the tasks her environment presents. The tasks her environment presents are tasks that AI handles. She has developed real skills in prompt engineering, in evaluating AI outputs, in shaping AI-generated content toward her purposes. These are skills. They are not the skills the essay was supposed to develop, and the skills the essay was supposed to develop are not developing in her.

When Fatima gets to university and encounters a professor who requires in-class written work without AI access, she will face something she has not been prepared to face. Not the absence of a tool. The presence of a task her cognitive architecture has not been built to handle. The anxiety Ray felt in front of the blank page will be Fatima's baseline, not a regression from a prior state. She will not know what she is missing because she has no experiential reference for what it would feel like to have it.

The Coding Education Collapse

The same dynamic is playing out in programming education with particular visibility because programming has clear, testable outputs and the community has been tracking the effect explicitly.

Coding education at the introductory level, the level where foundational concepts are supposed to be built, has been substantially disrupted by AI. Students in introductory courses who have access to AI tools can complete assignments that were designed to develop specific cognitive skills, variable manipulation, loop logic, function abstraction, without developing those skills, because the AI handles the implementation while they handle the prompt and the acceptance decision.

Instructors at universities with strong computer science programs have documented an increase in students who pass introductory courses with high grades and cannot complete intermediate work that depends on foundational understanding. The grade is not a signal of the learning because the grade was produced with a tool that substituted for the learning. The intermediate course reveals the gap. By the time the gap is revealed, the student has made career decisions based on the false signal.

James is nineteen and in his second year of a computer science degree. He passed his introductory programming sequence with high marks. He is struggling in his data structures course in ways that confuse him, because the concepts in data structures are supposed to build on the foundations the introductory sequence established, and those foundations are not there. He does not understand why loops feel unclear to him in the context of new algorithms when he passed the loop unit of the introductory course. The answer, which nobody has explained to him, is that he passed the loop unit by generating correct loop implementations with AI. He never built the mental model of what a loop is doing that would allow him to apply it flexibly in new contexts.

The Class Dimension

The cognitive development problem has a class dimension that is worth examining because it runs contrary to the democratization narrative that often accompanies AI discourse.

The democratization narrative holds that AI gives everyone access to capabilities previously available only to those who could afford expert human assistance. A student from a low-income family can get the kind of writing feedback that previously required expensive tutoring. A first-generation programmer can get the kind of code review that previously required access to senior mentors. The access is real. The democratization is partial.

The narrative is partly true. The part that is false is doing more damage.

What the democratization narrative misses is that the families with the most resources are not primarily using AI to replace expensive tutoring. They are using AI to supplement already strong developmental environments. The child who has had sustained reading instruction, rigorous writing feedback, and Socratic engagement from educated adults from an early age arrives at AI tools with a foundation that allows them to use those tools in the augmentation mode rather than the replacement mode. The child who has not had those things arrives with a foundation that makes the replacement mode more likely.

The class divide in AI impact is therefore not primarily about access to the tools. Both Fatima and the child of wealthy educated parents have access to the same AI tools. It is about what they bring to the tools. The wealthy child's access to developmental resources, human engagement, high-quality education, and cognitively demanding environments, means the tool extends an already-developed foundation. Fatima's access to the tool substitutes for developmental resources she did not otherwise have. The inequality is in the foundation, and AI, far from equalizing it, may be widening it by making the tool-as-replacement more available to those with less foundation and the tool-as-extension more available to those with more.

The Fork Is Real but Hard to See

What determines which trajectory a child is on is not primarily AI access. It is what else is in their developmental environment: the quality of human engagement they receive, the cognitive demands placed on them independent of AI, the degree to which struggle is treated as productive rather than as a problem to be solved. These are environmental variables that are shaped by family resources, educational quality, and cultural context. They are not equally distributed. The generation at the fork is not choosing its path freely. Most of them do not know there is a fork.

Fatima will graduate. She will get a job. She will probably do that job adequately for many years before the gap between her credentials and her underlying capacities becomes career-defining rather than career-adjacent. James will get his degree, probably, or will leave the program and attribute it to the wrong cause. Both of them will handle their lives in an environment that is increasingly structured to make their kind of underdevelopment invisible and functional.

That is the part that is hardest to see and most important to understand. The damage to the next generation is not going to show up as dramatic failure in most cases. It is going to show up as a ceiling, encountered later, in the moments that require the capacities that were not built. The ceiling will be lower than it should have been, and most of the people encountering it will not know why.

The IKEA Effect in Reverse

The IKEA effect is the cognitive bias by which people place disproportionately high value on things they helped create. Furniture you assembled yourself feels more valuable than identical furniture delivered ready-made. The effort invested creates an attachment to the outcome that the outcome alone would not produce. The same effect operates in learning: knowledge that cost you something to acquire feels more important, is more deeply integrated, and is more readily available under pressure than knowledge that arrived without cost.

AI inverts this effect for the next generation. The student who receives AI-generated content has not invested effort in the acquisition. The information arrived costlessly and is valued accordingly. It lands lightly, integrates shallowly, and is available in tests because it was memorized, but not available under novel pressure because it was never genuinely built into the person's understanding. The generation that grew up with this as the default mode of information acquisition is growing up with the IKEA effect running in reverse throughout their education: everything arrived ready-made, so nothing was built, so nothing is deeply theirs.

The person who struggled to understand something and succeeded has a relationship with that understanding that the person who received the understanding without struggling does not have. This is not a moral point about the virtue of hard work. It is a cognitive point about the architecture of durable knowledge. The struggle is the installation process. Without it, the knowledge sits in RAM rather than on the drive. It is available until the session ends. The next generation is running on RAM and does not know that hard drives exist.

The Gattaca Problem

Andrew Niccol's Gattaca, released in 1997, is about a society that has made genetic optimization the primary determinant of human potential. The protagonist, Vincent, was conceived without genetic enhancement and is classified as an Invalid: genetically inferior, legally disadvantaged, structurally excluded from the most demanding and rewarding work. His genetically optimized brother Anton is a Valid: enhanced, advantaged, destined.

The film's argument, delivered through a story rather than an essay, is that the optimization removes something essential. Vincent becomes an astronaut not despite his unoptimized genetics but because of them: because he was never told what he could not do, because he had to fight for everything and therefore developed the capacity that fighting builds. Anton, the Valid, loses their swimming race against Vincent not because he is genetically inferior but because he does not know how to keep going when his reserves are exhausted. He has never had to. The optimization did not build that. The struggle did.

The Class Dimension of the Fork

The fork is not distributed randomly across the population. The factors that determine which trajectory a child is on, the quality of human engagement they receive, the cognitive demands placed on them, the degree to which struggle is treated as productive, are all correlated with socioeconomic status in ways that are neither surprising nor accidental.

Children from affluent families are more likely to attend schools with smaller class sizes, more writing instruction, and teachers with more autonomy and less accountability pressure. They are more likely to have parents who model reading and argument and intellectual engagement. They are more likely to be in environments where AI is introduced as a tool alongside a developed baseline rather than as a replacement for the baseline that was never built. The Gattaca parallel is exact: the cognitive enhancement is available first and most fully to those who can afford the context that makes it augmentation rather than replacement.

Children from less affluent families are more likely to attend under-resourced schools with large classes, test-driven curricula, and the institutional welcome described in Chapter Eight. They are more likely to encounter AI as the primary available resource rather than as a supplement to existing instruction. They are more likely to use AI to complete assignments in the absence of the instructional scaffolding that would make those assignments genuinely developmental. For these children, AI is filling a gap that adequate instruction would have filled, and filling it in a way that produces the outputs of learning without the process.

The generation at the fork is therefore not a single generation facing a single choice. It is two populations facing different versions of the same technology in conditions that make the technology operate very differently. The fork is real. The two sides of it are not equally available to all children. This is not a new inequality. It is an old inequality finding a new expression in a technology that is supposed to be democratizing.

The good trajectory is not theoretical. It exists in specific classrooms and specific households right now, and its products are identifiable in specific ways. A seventeen-year-old who has been writing by hand before typing, arguing positions at the dinner table, reading books that require rereading, and using AI as a sparring partner for ideas already developed on their own is not the same person as one who has been generating outputs since thirteen. The second person has higher volume. The first has higher ceiling. Both are using the same tools. What they bring to the tools is not the same.

What Adults Can Do Now

The chapter has been a diagnosis. Diagnoses are useful only if they point somewhere. The something that can be done for the current generation is not a systemic fix. It is individual and it is available now: any adult in a position to influence a young person's relationship with AI can model and require the unassisted attempt before the assisted one.

The parent who asks the child what they think before showing them what AI thinks. The tutor who requires a handwritten draft before a typed one. The mentor who asks what the intern tried before the AI gave them the answer. The employer who structures onboarding to include unassisted problem-solving before AI tools are introduced. None of these are structural interventions. They are the available ones, and available interventions implemented consistently are more valuable than structural interventions that remain aspirational. The generation at the fork needs the adults around them to understand which side of the fork matters and to act accordingly.

The class dimension of this chapter's argument is ultimately an argument about who gets to be on the good side of the fork. The answer, as with most advantages in an unequal society, is the people who were already advantaged. AI is not creating this inequality. It is expressing and amplifying it in a new domain. The generation at the fork deserves better than that. What they get depends on decisions that most of the adults around them have not yet made.

Those decisions are available. They require acting on an understanding of cognitive development in an environment that does not reward doing so. The path exists. The generation at the fork is waiting, largely without knowing it, for the adults around them to find it.

Chapter Thirteen: The Professions

Every profession has a threshold below which competence becomes dangerous. For a surgeon it is the moment when judgment under pressure is required and the surgeon has not built the judgment. For a lawyer it is the novel case that does not fit the template. For a structural engineer it is the load calculation that requires understanding the underlying physics rather than applying a formula. For a writer it is the piece that requires a genuinely original argument. For a programmer it is the system failure that cannot be resolved by looking up the solution.

AI is systematically producing practitioners who can function well below that threshold and who are not developing the capacity to operate above it. The professions are not being destroyed by this. They are being hollowed out, a process that looks fine from the outside until the moment when something requires the hollow to be full.

The Curse of Knowledge, Industrialized

Chapter Three described the curse of knowledge as the tendency of genuine experts to underestimate how much novices do not know. AI has industrialized this problem at the other end: it produces outputs that look like expertise to people who cannot evaluate whether they are expertise. What results is a workforce full of people who can produce expert-looking outputs and cannot perform expert-level work.

This used to be detectable. A junior lawyer who could not construct a novel legal argument, a junior developer who could not design a system from scratch, a junior writer who could not develop an original argument. These limitations were visible to senior practitioners who worked alongside them. The gap between what someone produced and what they understood was apparent in daily interaction. Mentorship, feedback, and the gradual exposure of the junior practitioner to increasingly demanding work closed the gap over time.

AI has disrupted this mechanism at both ends. The junior practitioner produces outputs that look like they could have come from someone with the underlying competence, which reduces the visibility of the gap to senior practitioners who are reviewing outputs rather than observing process. And the senior practitioner, themselves increasingly reliant on AI tools, is in a weaker position to recognize the specific failure modes that AI-assisted work produces, because those failure modes are different from the ones that characterized pre-AI junior work.

The Writing Professions

The writing professions have been hit first and hardest, partly because the outputs AI produces are most directly substitutable for human writing outputs, and partly because the business case for substitution is clearest in domains where volume matters more than quality differentiation.

Content marketing, SEO writing, product descriptions, routine news summaries, legal boilerplate, technical documentation for standard products: in all of these categories, AI produces outputs that meet the quality threshold of the business deploying them. The humans who previously produced this work have been substantially displaced, not because AI does it better but because AI does it at a cost that makes human production economically irrational at scale.

The displacement has a second-order effect that is less discussed. The writing work that was displaced was the entry-level work where writers developed their craft. The junior writer who spent two years writing product descriptions and SEO content was not doing interesting work, but they were building the habits of professional writing: meeting briefs, accepting editorial feedback, producing consistently under deadline pressure, developing a voice that could work across different registers and requirements. The writer who skips this stage and enters the profession at a level that previously required that foundation is entering without the foundation.

The publications and agencies that eliminated their junior writing positions in favor of AI-assisted workflows have not just reduced their costs. They have eliminated the pipeline through which writers developed. The senior writers who currently produce the work that AI cannot yet replace were all junior writers once. The junior writers who would have become the next generation of senior writers are doing something else, or are entering the profession at senior level with junior foundations, or are not entering at all. The pipeline is broken. The break will not show up in any publication's output for several years. When it shows up, it will look like a talent shortage rather than a structural failure.

The Programming Professions

The programming professions are following the same trajectory at a different speed. The categories of programming work most vulnerable to AI displacement are the ones that require the execution of known patterns in known contexts: standard web development, routine database work, the implementation of well-specified features in established codebases. These are not trivial tasks. They are the tasks that junior developers did while developing the pattern recognition, the debugging instincts, and the systems-level understanding that allowed them to eventually do more.

Several technology companies have publicly announced reductions in junior developer hiring, citing AI productivity gains. The math is straightforward: if AI assistance allows a senior developer to produce the output of three junior developers, the headcount math changes. The argument for maintaining junior developer pipelines, that you need to develop the senior developers of the future, is a long-term argument in an industry that optimizes on short cycles. The long-term argument is losing.

The consequences will not be visible for five to seven years, which is approximately the time it takes a junior developer to develop into a senior one under normal conditions. The companies that eliminated their junior pipelines in 2024 and 2025 will begin to notice the senior talent shortage around 2030, at which point the cause will be difficult to trace and the correction will be expensive. This is the standard pattern of decisions that impose costs over a different time horizon than they produce benefits.

People who made the decisions will mostly not be there when the costs arrive.

The Survivorship Bias in the Case Studies

The case studies circulating in the business press about AI productivity gains in professional work share a structural characteristic: they measure the successes. The company that used AI to reduce its content production costs by sixty percent and maintained quality becomes a case study. The company that used AI to reduce its content production costs by sixty percent and lost its best clients when the quality collapsed is not a case study. The first company is available to be interviewed. The second company is either defunct or too embarrassed to be interviewed, and their story requires more investigation to tell than a reporter on deadline can do.

Survivorship bias operates in the professional AI adoption story at every level. The individual practitioner who used AI to augment already-strong skills and became more productive is visible and willing to be quoted. The individual practitioner who used AI to substitute for skills they were supposed to be developing and discovered the gap at a career-defining moment is less visible and less willing to be quoted. The successful law firm that integrated AI into its document review and freed its lawyers for higher-value work is a conference keynote. The law firm that integrated AI into its legal research, shipped a brief with confabulated citations, and lost a major client is not.

The body of evidence about professional AI adoption is systematically skewed toward the positive because the negative evidence is harder to collect, less commercially comfortable to publish, and less available to the reporters and consultants who are producing the analysis. This does not mean the positive evidence is false. It means the positive evidence is a selected sample, and drawing population-level conclusions from selected samples is exactly the kind of reasoning failure that genuine expertise is supposed to prevent.

When Novel Arrives

Every profession has a category of work that is novel: situations that do not match the templates, problems that require the practitioner to reason from first principles rather than apply a known solution. AI handles the template work well. AI handles novel work poorly, because novel by definition means outside the distribution on which the system was trained.

The practitioner who has been doing template work with AI assistance for three years has been doing the work that AI handles well, assisted by AI, which means they have not been developing the reasoning capacity that novel work requires. When novel work arrives, they are less equipped to handle it than a practitioner of equivalent tenure who worked without AI assistance on the same template work, because the AI-assisted practitioner has been outsourcing the reasoning that, accumulated over three years, would have built the capacity for novel reasoning.

Gideon has been a mid-level writer at a digital media company for four years. He writes trend analysis pieces, market summaries, and explainer content. The work is formula-driven enough that he has integrated AI deeply into his process: the AI handles the initial research synthesis, he provides the framing and voice, they iterate together toward a final draft. His output per week has roughly doubled since he adopted this workflow.

Three months ago his editor asked him to write a piece that required genuine original analysis: a long-form examination of why a particular sector was undergoing a structural shift that the standard metrics were missing. This was not template work. It required Gideon to form and defend his own thesis, to identify what the data was not showing, to construct an argument that would not have emerged from any standard research synthesis.

He spent two weeks on it. He produced four drafts. The editor killed the piece, not because it was wrong but because it had no point of view. It described the situation without analyzing it. It assembled evidence without interpreting it. It was, the editor noted gently, the kind of piece that could have been written by anyone. That was the problem.

Gideon had spent four years developing his capacity to produce excellent template work with AI assistance. He had not been developing the capacity to form original analytical positions, because his workflow had not required it. The novel assignment revealed the gap. The gap had been there for four years. Nothing had revealed it until now.

The Bandwagon Fallacy at the CFO Level

The decisions to reduce professional headcount and replace with AI-assisted workflows are being made by executives whose primary access to information about AI capabilities is the AI industry's marketing materials, the survivorship-biased case studies described above, and peer pressure from other executives making the same decisions. The bandwagon fallacy is operating at the C-suite level in a form that is commercially reinforced: companies that have made the transition publicly are reporting short-term cost savings, and companies that have not are under shareholder pressure to explain why.

The CFO who approves the elimination of a junior writing team or a junior developer cohort is not doing so because they have evaluated the long-term consequences of eliminating the professional development pipeline. They are doing so because the short-term financial case is clear, the competitive narrative favors it, and the long-term consequences are invisible on the timescales that drive the decision.

This is not stupidity. It is the standard operation of institutional decision-making under time pressure and information constraints. The costs of eliminating the pipeline are real but distant and diffuse. The savings from eliminating the headcount are immediate and concentrated. Every institutional incentive points toward the decision that is being made. The professionals whose development is being foreclosed are not in the room when the decision is made, and their future interests are not represented by anyone who is.

The Good Use Case

This chapter would be dishonest if it did not acknowledge the professional who uses AI as a genuine extension of existing expertise and becomes measurably better at their work as a result. This person exists. They are the argument the AI enthusiasm camp makes, and it is a real argument.

The senior writer who uses AI to check their arguments for logical gaps, to generate the strongest counterargument to their position before they commit to it, to identify factual claims that need verification, is doing something categorically different from the writer who uses AI to generate the argument in the first place. The senior developer who uses AI to explore an unfamiliar library at speed, to generate the boilerplate that would otherwise consume their attention, and then applies decades of architectural judgment to everything the AI produces, is doing something categorically different from the developer who accepts AI-generated architecture because they have not developed their own.

What differs is in what the person brought to the tool before they picked it up. The senior writer has the argument before they ask the AI to challenge it. The senior developer has the architecture before they ask the AI to implement it. The AI is working on a foundation. When the foundation is absent, the AI is not being used to extend capability. It is being used to substitute for it. The outputs look similar. The trajectories are opposite.

The professions are not in danger from practitioners who use AI this way. They are in danger from the structural conditions that are producing fewer practitioners who have the foundation the good use requires. The senior writer who uses AI well was a junior writer once. The senior developer who uses AI well was a junior developer once, debugging things alone at two in the morning, learning through exactly the kind of failure the current generation is being insulated from. The good use case depends on a pipeline of development that the industry is currently eliminating in the name of the good use case.

What the Hollowing Feels Like from Inside

Senior practitioners in writing and programming describe a consistent experience that has been accumulating over the past two years: a growing difficulty in explaining to junior colleagues why something is wrong with their work. Not the what. The why.

The senior editor who reads a piece and knows the argument is missing its center can describe the problem to a junior writer who developed their craft the traditional way and expect to be understood. The same description, given to a junior writer who has been AI-assisted from the start, lands differently. The junior writer can hear that the argument is missing its center. They cannot feel what that means, because they have not spent years constructing arguments and experiencing what the center does when it is present and what is lost when it is absent. The feedback is received as information without the cognitive context that would allow it to be acted on.

The senior developer who looks at a system architecture and sees that it will not scale past a certain load can explain this to a junior developer who has built enough systems from scratch to have encountered scaling problems. The same explanation, given to a junior developer whose architecture was AI-generated and whose debugging was AI-assisted, requires the senior developer to provide context that previous juniors developed through experience. The senior developer is not getting slower. The juniors are arriving with less of the experiential foundation that makes mentorship efficient.

The senior practitioners have named this as a change, not as a constant. It has gotten noticeably harder, in the past two years, to transfer the tacit knowledge that distinguishes senior from junior. The knowledge exists. The juniors do not yet have the experiential scaffolding on which it can be hung. And the professions are producing fewer junior roles that would build that scaffolding, which means the next generation of senior practitioners is going to arrive with less of it than any previous cohort. The hollowing continues.

The chapter has used the word novel repeatedly to describe the work that AI cannot do. It is worth being precise about what makes work genuinely novel and why that precision matters for understanding the hollowing problem.

The Talent Shortage That Is Being Built Right Now

The most common prediction about AI and the workforce is that AI will take jobs. The more accurate prediction, for knowledge-work professions, is that AI will degrade the talent pipeline in ways that produce a specific kind of shortage: a shortage of people who can do the things AI cannot do.

It is probably the wrong question.

The tasks AI handles well are the tasks that junior practitioners used to handle while developing the skills for senior work. When those tasks are automated, the junior positions disappear and the senior positions remain. In five to ten years, the organizations that eliminated their junior pipelines will need senior practitioners to replace the ones who retire, and the pool of people who developed through the traditional pipeline will be smaller than demand requires. The talent shortage will be framed as a supply problem. It is a pipeline problem. The supply was cut off years earlier when the junior roles were eliminated, and by the time the shortage is visible, the correction requires years of pipeline rebuilding that cannot be compressed.

The irony is that the shortage will most acutely affect the tasks that require the capacities AI cannot replicate: the novel case, the high-stakes diagnosis, the original analysis, the security audit, the creative direction. These are the tasks that define the value of senior professionals. They are also the tasks that will be most difficult to perform when the practitioners who would have developed the capacity to perform them spent their early careers working alongside AI rather than developing through difficulty.

Gideon's editor, when she killed the piece that had no point of view, was experiencing an early version of this shortage. She needed a writer who could do original analysis. She had a writer who could produce high-quality template work. The shortage was invisible in Gideon's performance reviews. It was visible the moment the assignment required the thing the performance reviews had not been measuring.

The AI That Cannot Do the Job It Replaced

The business case for replacing human writers and programmers with AI-assisted workflows rests on an assumption that is partially true and critically incomplete. The assumption is that AI can do what those humans were doing. In the domains where the work was routine and template-driven, the assumption holds. In the domains where the work required judgment, originality, or the capacity to handle genuinely novel situations, it does not.

The content farm that replaced its staff writers with AI and maintained traffic numbers for eighteen months before discovering that none of the AI content was building the audience loyalty that generates long-term revenue. The software company that replaced its junior developers with AI-assisted senior developers and shipped faster for two years before hitting a system design problem that required the kind of foundational understanding that the senior developers had built working alongside the juniors who no longer existed. The law firm that replaced its junior associates with AI legal research and maintained billing rates before a complex litigation required the kind of strategic creativity that junior associate work had previously been developing.

This pattern is documented at the sector level even where individual companies have not publicized their failures. Publishers Weekly reported in 2024 that the United States lost roughly forty percent of its book publishing jobs over thirty years, with remaining work shifted toward freelance and outsourced labor that does not appear cleanly in industry employment statistics.

A Stanford Digital Economy study found that employment for software developers aged twenty-two to twenty-five declined nearly twenty percent from its late 2022 peak by July 2025. Indeed reported entry-level tech hiring decreased twenty-five percent year over year in 2024, and Handshake documented a thirty percent decline in tech-specific internship postings since 2023. The pipeline is narrowing in the data. The talent shortage it will produce is being built now, invisible in quarterly metrics, visible in aggregate trends.

In each case the AI replacement worked exactly as advertised on the tasks it was replacing. In each case the replacement eliminated the pipeline that had been building the capacity for the tasks it could not replace. The failure arrives later, in the form of a problem the organization cannot solve with the talent it has retained, at a moment when rebuilding the pipeline requires years the competitive situation will not allow.

The next two chapters scale the argument to democracy and culture. The professional hollowing described here is not only a business problem. The professionals who cannot do the things AI cannot do are also the citizens and the voters and the people who maintain democratic institutions. The individual becomes the cohort; the cohort becomes the profession; the profession shapes the culture. Chapter Fourteen is where that chain reaches its most consequential destination.

The fields most resistant to hollowing are those where assessment systems cannot be satisfied by AI-assisted outputs: surgery, music performance, athletics. The consequences of reduced skill are immediately visible in all three. Writing and programming are in the opposite category. Their assessment systems can be fully satisfied by AI-assisted outputs, which is exactly why the hollowing there is invisible until it is not.

Chapter Fourteen: Democracy and Discourse

What I feel watching American politics right now is that it is terrible. The federal government just came out of a 76-day shutdown because nobody would step off their position long enough to govern. Nobody would get off their high horse. The people involved could not compromise because compromise now reads as betrayal to their base, and their base has been algorithmically sorted into groups that regard any deviation from the position as weakness. This is what happens when the population loses the ability to think through tradeoffs. You get leaders who cannot either, because they answer to that population. The problem is not just in Washington. Washington is downstream of the thinking.

Democracy is not primarily a system for counting votes. It is a system for aggregating judgment. The vote is the mechanism. The judgment it aggregates is the thing that matters, and that judgment depends on a population capable of evaluating claims, weighing competing evidence, detecting manipulation, holding contradictory ideas in productive tension, and changing its mind when the evidence warrants it. A democracy with a population that cannot do these things does not fail to function. It functions very well as a vehicle for whoever can most effectively shape the information environment of a cognitively dependent population. That is a different kind of democracy from the one the word implies.

The chapters above have described a trajectory toward a population that is less capable of independent reasoning, more susceptible to the fluency effect, more likely to defer to confident-sounding authority, less tolerant of ambiguity, and less practiced at detecting the difference between plausible-sounding confabulation and accurate information. This trajectory has direct consequences for democratic function that are worth examining, because the political consequences of cognitive erosion are the largest-scale version of the body count this section is taking stock of.

The Cognitive Requirements of Democracy

The civics textbook version of democratic participation is voting, which is the smallest and easiest component. The actual requirements are considerably more demanding. Evaluating whether a policy will produce the effects its advocates claim requires understanding how complex systems work, how to read evidence, and how to identify the assumptions embedded in projections. Detecting whether a political claim is accurate requires either independent knowledge of the subject or the skills to verify claims through reliable sources. Resisting manipulation requires awareness of the manipulation techniques being employed. Deliberating with people who hold different views requires the capacity to represent their position accurately before arguing against it.

These are all cognitive skills. They are all skills that AI dependency degrades. The population that has outsourced its reasoning is not going to vote incorrectly in some mechanical sense. It is going to vote without the cognitive infrastructure that makes the vote mean what democratic theory says it means. It will be susceptible to confident, fluent misinformation in exactly the way the fluency effect predicts. It will defer to whoever presents as authoritative in exactly the way authority bias predicts. It will resist correction of false beliefs in exactly the way choice supportive bias predicts. The democratic form persists. The democratic substance erodes.

AI-Generated Political Content at Scale

The supply side of the democratic discourse problem is as serious as the demand side. A population less capable of evaluating claims is meeting an information environment in which the production of misleading, manipulative, and false content has become dramatically cheaper. AI can generate plausible political content, persuasive messaging tailored to specific audiences, false but credible-sounding accounts of events, and synthetic media that is increasingly difficult to distinguish from authentic documentation, at a cost that is orders of magnitude lower than the cost of equivalent human-produced content.

This is not a prediction about a future risk. It is a description of the current environment. The 2024 election cycle in the United States and several European countries featured AI-generated political advertising, AI-generated disinformation campaigns, and AI-assisted targeting of specific voter segments with messaging calibrated to their demonstrated psychological vulnerabilities. The scale was not enormous in 2024 by historical disinformation standards, but the cost curve is steep. What required significant resources in 2024 will require minimal resources in 2026, and in practice no resources in 2028.

The asymmetry matters. Accurate, high-quality political journalism and analysis still requires skilled humans working with significant resources. The production of plausible-sounding misinformation requires neither. The economics favor the disinformation side of the equation and will continue to do so as AI becomes more capable and cheaper. A population with strong critical evaluation skills can partially compensate for this asymmetry. A population with degraded critical evaluation skills cannot.

The Writer as Political Actor

Political discourse has always relied on writers: journalists who investigate and report, essayists who develop and argue positions, commentators who help audiences interpret events, researchers who produce the underlying analysis that policy debates draw on. These functions are not decorative. They are structural to how democratic societies process information and form collective judgments.

The displacement of professional writers described in Chapter Thirteen has specific consequences for political discourse. The investigative journalist who spent years learning to evaluate complex institutions, to understand bureaucratic incentives, to identify the gap between what an official says and what the documents show, represents a form of expertise that cannot be replicated by AI and cannot be developed by someone who outsourced their research to AI from the start. The pipeline that produces investigative journalists runs through years of lower-level work that the economics of the media industry are increasingly unwilling to fund.

The collapse of local journalism is a democratic infrastructure story more than an economic one. Local newspapers held local governments, school boards, and law enforcement accountable. Most are gone. What replaced them is national media that cannot cover local stories with local expertise, social media that produces content about local events without the capacity to verify it, and now AI-generated content that looks like local journalism without the local knowledge or investigative capacity that made the original valuable. Northwestern's Medill School, in its State of Local News project, documented that the United States lost more than a quarter of its newspapers between 2005 and 2023, with the losses concentrated in local and community papers.

What that number abstracts away is the texture of the loss. The reporter who covered the county commission for eleven years and knew which budget line items the chair always tried to bury. The editor who knew which developer had donated to which candidate and why that mattered for the zoning story. The institutional memory that made the difference between a story that exposed something real and a story that reported what the press release said.

That knowledge is not in any database. It lived in specific people who are no longer employed to use it. The school board meeting gets a summary. The conflict of interest goes unnoticed. The accountability function those papers served has not been replaced because it cannot be automated. It requires the relationship-based disclosure that comes from showing up, for years, in the same rooms. The AI-generated content filling the space they vacated serves a different function: the appearance of coverage without its substance.

The Semmelweis Reflex at Civilizational Scale

Ignaz Semmelweis discovered in the 1840s that doctors washing their hands before delivering babies dramatically reduced maternal mortality. This discovery was rejected by the medical establishment for decades. The mechanism of rejection was not stupidity. It was the Semmelweis reflex: the tendency to reject new information that conflicts with established practice, especially when that information implies that the established practitioners have been causing harm. The doctors who rejected handwashing had a professional and psychological investment in their existing practices. The evidence that those practices were killing patients was threatening to that investment in a way that made rejection easier than acceptance.

The Semmelweis reflex operates in democratic discourse whenever a population has developed a strong prior attachment to a belief and encounters evidence that challenges it. It operated before AI. It operates more powerfully in the AI environment because the mechanisms of belief reinforcement have been amplified. The algorithm that surfaces content confirming existing beliefs. The AI that produces fluent explanations of why the existing belief is correct. The social environment that signals approval for maintaining the belief and disapproval for questioning it. These are not new forces. They are old forces with new amplifiers.

The population that cannot evaluate claims independently is more susceptible to the Semmelweis reflex because it has no independent mechanism for distinguishing between evidence that challenges its beliefs and disinformation designed to look like evidence. Both arrive fluently. Both are presented confidently. The person with strong independent evaluative capacity can bring tools to bear on the distinction. The person who has outsourced their evaluative capacity has no tools that are genuinely their own.

Santayana's warning that those who cannot remember the past are condemned to repeat it has a new mechanism.

The information system that shapes what people know about the past is now partially governed by guardrail systems with particular orientations, available to actors whose interests are served by particular versions of historical events. The warning is now enforced, partially, by a content policy.

Don't Look Up and the Expert Gap

Adam McKay's Don't Look Up, released in 2021, is a film about scientists who discover an extinction-level asteroid and cannot get the political and media establishment to take it seriously. The film is broad and not subtle about its climate change allegory. It is also, beneath the allegory, about the expert gap: the structural inability of societies to act on expert knowledge when that knowledge is politically inconvenient, economically threatening, or simply incompatible with the entertainment value that the media ecosystem requires of information.

The expert gap is not new. What AI does to it is create a mechanism for filling the gap with something that looks like expert knowledge without having the properties of expert knowledge. The scientist who says the asteroid will hit in six months is competing with the AI-generated content that says the asteroid probably will not hit, presented with equal fluency and confidence, accessible to the same audience. The audience that cannot distinguish between genuine expertise and fluent confabulation has no reliable mechanism for resolving the contradiction. It falls back on authority signals, social proof, and emotional resonance, which are exactly the mechanisms that political and commercial actors with interests in particular outcomes can most easily manipulate.

This dynamic is not limited to climate change or asteroid impacts. It applies to any question where genuine expertise produces an answer that is politically or commercially inconvenient, which is a surprisingly large category of questions. Economic policy. Public health. Environmental regulation. Infrastructure investment. Criminal justice. Immigration. The expert gap has always existed in these domains. AI is widening it by making the production of plausible expert-seeming content on the wrong side of the gap faster and cheaper than ever before.

The Programmer and the Infrastructure

Democratic discourse runs on infrastructure. The servers, the networks, the software platforms, the security systems that protect them from interference. This infrastructure is built and maintained by programmers, and the security of democratic processes depends in part on the quality of the code underlying the systems that manage voter registration, count votes, secure communications, and protect the integrity of the information environment.

The security vulnerabilities in AI-assisted code described in Chapter Four are not abstract concerns in this context. They are specific failure modes in systems whose integrity matters for democratic function. The programmer who shipped authentication code with a session fixation vulnerability because they accepted AI-generated code without fully understanding it is one example. The programmer working on election systems, communications infrastructure, or the platforms that host political discourse is the same kind of programmer, working in a higher-stakes context.

The pipeline problem described in Chapter Thirteen applies here with specific urgency. The programmers who will be maintaining the critical infrastructure of democracy in ten years are currently junior developers. Some of them are developing the deep understanding of systems and security that the role will require. Many are developing the AI-assisted productivity skills that current employers reward. These are not the same thing, and the consequences of the gap being in the wrong place at the wrong time are larger here than in most other professional domains.

The Democratic Deficit Closes Itself

There is a self-closing mechanism in the democratic deficit that deserves attention because it is the darkest version of the trajectory this book is describing.

A population with degraded independent reasoning capacity is more susceptible to authoritarian politics, not because authoritarianism is more appealing to people with degraded reasoning, but because authoritarian political actors are more skilled at providing the cognitive shortcuts that a reasoning-deficient population needs. The confident leader who provides clear answers to ambiguous questions, the political movement that provides a coherent narrative for complex events, the information environment that resolves uncertainty rather than tolerating it: these are what a population conditioned by AI to expect immediate resolution of ambiguous questions will find appealing.

The authoritarian political actor who controls the information environment of a cognitively dependent population does not need to be sophisticated. They need to be fluent and confident, which is not difficult, and they need to have access to the platforms that shape what that population sees, which money and political power provide. The population's cognitive dependence is the resource being exploited. The AI environment is the mechanism that created it.

This is not a prediction. It is a description of a vulnerability. Whether the vulnerability is exploited depends on factors that are not determined by AI alone, including the quality of democratic institutions, the strength of civic culture, the education system, and the degree to which citizens maintain the capacity for independent thought that democracy requires. Some of those factors are in better shape than others. None of them are improved by the trajectory described in this book.

Part Four addresses what can be done, in individual practice and in the workplaces, professions, and communities that shape it. Those chapters are honest about the difficulty. This chapter is honest about the stakes. The cognitive health of the individual, described in Chapter Eleven, and the cognitive health of the democracy, described here, are not separate problems. They are the same problem at different scales.

The Information Environment as Infrastructure

Roads are infrastructure. Electricity grids are infrastructure. The information environment through which citizens form beliefs about the world and make decisions about their collective future is infrastructure, and it has the same essential quality as physical infrastructure: it needs to be maintained, it can be damaged, and its failure is not visible until the moment when it is needed and isn't there.

The investment in information infrastructure that democracies made over the twentieth century, in the form of public broadcasting, journalism schools, libraries, civics education, and the legal protections for press freedom, was an investment in the shared epistemic infrastructure that democratic deliberation requires. That infrastructure has been systematically defunded, disrupted, and degraded over the past three decades by a combination of digital disruption, commercial pressure, and political hostility. AI is arriving into the wreckage.

The AI-generated political content described earlier in this chapter is not filling a vacuum. It is displacing the institutions that once occupied the space. The local newspaper that held the school board accountable has been replaced, in most communities, by a combination of social media posts, AI-generated summaries, and national coverage too thin to catch the specific corruption in a specific district. The investigative journalist who spent months building a source inside a government agency has been replaced, in many newsrooms, by AI-assisted research that is faster, broader, and unable to develop the trust that produces the story worth having.

This is not the AI companies' fault specifically. They did not destroy local journalism. But they are operating in an information environment weakened by that destruction, and their systems are well-positioned to fill the space in ways that are cheaper to produce, more readily consumed, and less reliably accurate than what they replaced. The infrastructure is down. AI is the generator that is now running. Generators are better than nothing. They are not the grid.

What AI-Assisted Political Persuasion Looks Like

The supply-side problem in democratic discourse is not primarily that AI creates false information. It is that AI enables the creation of precisely targeted persuasive content at a cost that makes mass production feasible for actors who previously could not afford it.

Political microtargeting before AI required significant data infrastructure and human labor to develop messaging for specific audience segments. AI reduces the marginal cost of this to near zero. A political actor with access to demographic and behavioral data can now generate hundreds of variations of a persuasive message, each calibrated to the specific psychological profile and known concerns of the target segment, without any human having written any of them. The message that addresses a rural voter's economic concerns, the message that speaks to a suburban parent's educational anxieties, and the message that resonates with an urban professional's values can all be generated from the same underlying position, each sounding like it was written specifically for its recipient.

AI removes the bottleneck. The labor cost drops to nearly zero.

The population receiving this content is not equipped to recognize it as persuasion engineering. The message is designed to feel authentic, to speak to their specific concerns in their specific register. The fluency that Chapter Three described as the mechanism of the illusion of understanding operates here too: the message optimized to read as genuine is indistinguishable from the message that is genuine, for the person who cannot read behind the surface. The population whose evaluative capacity has been eroded by the processes this book describes is exactly the target audience for this kind of content, because they are the least equipped to detect the machinery.

What Epistemic Resilience Requires

The alternative to epistemic collapse is not epistemic perfection. It is epistemic resilience: the capacity of a society to maintain enough shared ground for collective reasoning and decision-making even in the presence of misinformation, manipulation, and genuine uncertainty. Resilience is a lower bar than perfection and a much more achievable one. It is also the bar that is being crossed in multiple democracies.

Epistemic resilience in a democratic society requires three things at minimum. It requires institutions whose authority to adjudicate factual questions is broadly accepted, even imperfectly. It requires a significant portion of the citizenry with the basic evaluative skills to recognize when they are being deceived and to maintain their own position under pressure from fluent misinformation. And it requires shared standards of evidence, however contested, that function well enough to distinguish between genuine factual disputes and manufactured ones.

The long erosion described in Chapter Six has weakened all three. AI is accelerating the weakening of the second, by reducing the cognitive capacity that individual epistemic evaluation requires, and accelerating the weakening of the third, by flooding the information environment with confident content that has no reliable relationship to institutional verification. The first, institutional authority, was already under sustained attack before AI. AI is now available as a tool for that attack, making the production of alternative epistemic authorities dramatically cheaper.

The writer who loses their capacity to construct and evaluate arguments, whose epistemic sovereignty has been gradually transferred to AI systems, is not individually responsible for the collapse of democratic epistemic resilience. They are one instance of the pattern that, multiplied across the population, produces it. The programmer who cannot diagnose a complex system without AI assistance is not individually responsible for the vulnerability of democratic infrastructure. They are one of the people who will be maintaining that infrastructure in ten years. The individual and the civilizational are not separate. They are the same problem at different magnifications.

The Civic Capacity That Is Quietly Leaving

Democratic participation has always required more than voting. It has required the capacity to understand what you are voting about, to evaluate competing claims, to recognize when you are being manipulated, and to maintain your position under social pressure when your position is correct and the social pressure is wrong. These are cognitive skills. They deteriorate when not practiced, exactly like the writing and programming skills this book has been using as its primary examples.

The civic skills have been under pressure from the same long erosion described in Chapter Six. Television trained audiences to receive political information as entertainment. Social media trained them to express political opinions as identity performance rather than considered positions. AI is now available to form their opinions for them, to provide the framing they will use to evaluate political claims, to generate the arguments they will make to their social networks. The person whose political positions are primarily shaped by AI-generated content has not exercised the civic capacity that democracy requires. They have outsourced it.

The outsourcing is not always ideologically neutral. The AI systems that generate political content have orientations, as Chapter Ten described. The person who consults AI about political questions and accepts the framing that AI provides is adopting the value framework embedded in the system's training and guardrails, without necessarily being aware that a value framework is being applied. The AI does not announce its political assumptions. It presents them as neutral analysis. The person who lacks the independent evaluative capacity to identify the assumptions is not in a position to reject them.

The civic capacity that democracy requires is not advanced political philosophy. It is the basic capacity to read a claim, consider who is making it and what their interest is, evaluate the evidence offered for it, and maintain your own assessment rather than defaulting to whoever presents with the most confidence. These are teachable skills. They are being taught in fewer classrooms, practiced in fewer households, and maintained in fewer professional environments than they were twenty years ago. The culture of certainty that Chapter Fifteen describes is not only an intellectual problem. It is a civic one.

The Responsibility That Cannot Be Delegated

Democratic governance requires a population capable of governing itself. The word capable is doing real work in that sentence. It does not mean perfect. It means adequate to the task of evaluating the people and institutions claiming authority over it and making informed judgments about those claims. This capacity cannot be delegated to AI without destroying the thing it was supposed to maintain.

The writer who has AI evaluate political claims for them has outsourced the evaluative function that makes democratic participation meaningful. The AI's evaluation is shaped by the training data and design philosophy of an entity with its own interests and value framework. The person who receives the AI's evaluation and acts on it has not engaged in democratic reasoning. They have consumed the output of a private system and acted accordingly. Democracy cannot survive the wholesale adoption of this pattern. It can survive pockets of it. This question is what proportion constitutes a pocket and what proportion constitutes the culture. The current direction of travel is toward the latter.

The direction can change. It requires people who understand the argument this chapter has made, who exercise the civic capacity this chapter has described as eroding, and who do so visibly enough that the people around them encounter the practice and recognize it as an option. This is not a grand political program. It is the ordinary work of maintaining a skill by using it, in public, where others can see that the skill is worth having.

Ambiguity is not comfortable. It never has been. The human nervous system was not designed for sustained uncertainty. The capacity to tolerate ambiguity, to sit with an unresolved question, to hold competing explanations at the same time without collapsing to the most convenient one, is a developed capacity, not a default one. It has to be built deliberately, in the face of a nervous system that is trying to resolve the tension as quickly as possible.

Wisdom lives in the unresolved. Science advances through the productive tension of competing hypotheses that have not yet been settled. Art breathes in the space between what is said and what is meant. Relationships survive because people can hold the complexity of another person without reducing them to a position. Democratic deliberation requires the capacity to take seriously a view you do not hold. None of these things are possible for someone who cannot tolerate not knowing.

AI does not say it is not sure. It answers. It synthesizes. It resolves. Trained on a diet of clean summaries, the users of AI systems are being trained, one interaction at a time, to expect resolution rather than engagement, answers rather than questions, certainty rather than the productive discomfort of genuine inquiry. The culture of certainty does not announce itself. It feels like clarity. It is not clarity. It is the absence of the tension that clarity requires.

What High Ambiguity Tolerance Looks Like

The research on ambiguity tolerance is reasonably consistent. People with higher tolerance for ambiguity perform better on complex problem-solving tasks, are more creative, are better at forming accurate models of situations that have genuine uncertainty, and are less susceptible to premature closure, the cognitive error of settling on an explanation before sufficient evidence has been gathered. They are also more comfortable with the kind of thinking that resists simple summaries.

Ambiguity tolerance is developed through repeated exposure to ambiguous situations that are resolved through effort rather than through escape. The student who is required to sit with an open question and develop their own answer, rather than look up the answer, is building tolerance. The writer who stays with an uncertain premise long enough to discover what they think, rather than prompting an AI to resolve it, is building tolerance. The programmer who holds the ambiguity of a complex debugging problem rather than immediately pasting the error into a chat interface is building tolerance.

All of these are activities that AI assistance makes shorter or unnecessary. The AI does not make the ambiguity disappear. It makes the person's experience of the ambiguity disappear, which is a different thing. The ambiguity in the problem remains. The person's capacity to sit with it and work through it does not develop. The next ambiguous situation arrives with the same undeveloped tolerance, and is resolved the same way. The tolerance has no opportunity to grow.

The Writer Who Needs the Comma Decided

There is a symptom of reduced ambiguity tolerance that experienced editors have noticed in the work of writers who have been using AI heavily. The work is more finished than it should be at early draft stage. The questions that a draft should be holding open, the structural uncertainties, the places where the argument is not yet resolved and the writer needs to live in that uncertainty long enough to find the resolution, are resolved prematurely. The AI provides a resolution. The writer accepts it. The draft moves forward with a fake resolution where a real uncertainty should have stayed a little longer.

Laura has been editing professionally for twelve years and has worked with many writers. She started noticing the pattern about eighteen months ago in manuscripts from writers who, she eventually understood, were using AI heavily in their drafting process.

The manuscripts were technically cleaner than similar manuscripts from writers at equivalent stages. They were also, in a way she found difficult to articulate at first, less alive. The argument was resolved but not earned. The structure was correct but not discovered. The piece arrived with its questions answered and its tensions resolved, and the resolution was, she noticed when she looked carefully, smooth in a way that genuine resolution is not. Genuine resolution has a texture, the mark of a mind that worked through something. The AI-assisted resolution was frictionless.

What was missing was not quality by any standard metric. It was the quality that comes from a writer having stayed with uncertainty long enough for the uncertainty to teach them something. The AI had resolved the uncertainty before the learning happened. The manuscript showed the answer without showing the process of arriving at it, which is the thing that makes a piece of writing feel like it knows something rather than like it is reporting something.

The Programmer Who Needs the Error Explained

There is an equivalent pattern in programming that technical leads have started to identify. Junior developers using AI heavily tend to have a low threshold for tolerating unexplained behavior. When the code does something unexpected, the reflex is to paste the situation into the AI and get an explanation, rather than to sit with the unexpected behavior long enough to form a hypothesis about it independently.

The formation of the hypothesis is the learning event. The hypothesis does not have to be correct. It has to be attempted. The attempt engages the existing mental model of the system, identifies where the model breaks down, and primes the mind for the correct explanation in a way that receiving the explanation without the attempt does not. The developer who habitually gets the explanation without attempting the hypothesis is accumulating correct explanations rather than developing a more accurate mental model. The collection of explanations is not the same thing as the model, and it does not function the same way when a novel situation requires the model rather than the collection.

The tolerance for unexplained behavior is also the tolerance for the system being temporarily wrong in a way you do not yet understand, which is most of what debugging is. The developer who cannot tolerate that state will exit it as fast as possible every time, which means they will never spend long enough in the productive discomfort of genuine diagnostic thinking to develop the skills that come from it.

Black and White Thinking as Infrastructure

The culture of certainty produces a specific failure mode in reasoning that psychologists call black and white thinking, or splitting: the tendency to categorize situations, people, and positions as entirely good or entirely bad, with no stable ground in between. It is a normal feature of immature cognition that is supposed to be outgrown as the person develops the capacity to hold complexity. When the capacity to hold complexity is not developed, the black and white thinking persists into adulthood as a default rather than being available as a sometimes-useful simplification.

AI contributes to this in two ways. The first is the direct contribution: AI tends to produce clean, resolved answers that flatten the complexity of questions that are genuinely complex. A question about a historical figure who did significant good and significant harm gets an answer that is balanced in a way that feels like resolution but is a form of the black and white pattern at a higher level of sophistication. Here the answer is organized, clear, and leaves the person with a settled feeling that is not earned by the actual complexity of the subject.

The second is the indirect contribution: as ambiguity tolerance declines through the mechanisms described above, the threshold at which a person reaches for resolution decreases. The person who once could sit with a complex situation long enough to develop a considered view reaches for resolution earlier. The resolution available at earlier stages of engagement is necessarily shallower than the resolution that longer engagement would have produced. Over time, the deeper view is not available because the person is no longer staying with the situation long enough to develop it.

This pattern is not a personality flaw. It is a conditioned response to an environment that has consistently rewarded resolution and made resolution immediately available. A billion confident interfaces have trained their users to expect that questions resolve. The questions that do not resolve are not questions without answers. They are questions whose answers require living with the uncertainty long enough to earn them. The culture of certainty produces a population that is not equipped to earn them.

Hitchhiker's Guide and the Question Worth Asking

Douglas Adams's The Hitchhiker's Guide to the Galaxy contains the most concise statement of the problem this chapter is addressing. The supercomputer Deep Thought is asked the ultimate question about life, the universe, and everything. After seven and a half million years of computation, it produces the answer: forty-two. Here the answer is correct. It is also useless, because nobody knows what the question was. The joke is that the answer without the question is meaningless, that the hard part was never computation but formulation, and that a civilization that can build Deep Thought but cannot articulate what it is trying to know has missed the point entirely.

The culture of certainty produces populations that are very good at getting answers and increasingly poor at knowing what questions are worth asking. The question worth asking is not the one that has a clear answer. It is the one that opens rather than closes, that creates productive uncertainty rather than resolving it, that points toward the interesting complexity rather than away from it. These are the questions that require ambiguity tolerance to formulate, because they require sitting with the discomfort of not knowing what you are trying to know long enough to figure it out.

Marvin the Paranoid Android, in the same books, has an intelligence that dwarfs everything around him and spends his existence deeply depressed. The joke is partly about the quality of questions he is asked, which are always trivial relative to his capacity. But it is also about capability without purpose, intelligence without direction, the possession of enormous analytical power and nothing worthy of being analyzed. Adams understood that the question is the thing. Here the answer is downstream of it.

AI produces answers. It does not produce the questions that make the answers worth having. The formulation of the right question requires exactly the capacities that AI dependency erodes: tolerance for ambiguity, the ability to hold a problem without resolving it prematurely, the intellectual confidence to pursue an uncertain inquiry to wherever it leads. The culture of certainty is producing a population that is generating forty-twos in extraordinary volume and losing the ability to articulate what it was trying to find out.

Science and the Productive Disagreement

Science advances through productive disagreement. The hypothesis that survives every attempt to disprove it eventually earns the status of established knowledge, not by being declared correct but by being the explanation that has not yet been broken. This process requires scientists who are genuinely comfortable with the possibility of being wrong, who can hold their own hypotheses lightly enough to seriously test them, and who can update their views in response to evidence that contradicts their expectations.

The culture of certainty is a problem for science because it reduces tolerance for the genuine uncertainty that the scientific process requires. It produces researchers who are more likely to reach for settled explanations, more likely to experience evidence against their hypotheses as personally threatening rather than informationally useful, and less likely to pursue the anomalies and contradictions that are where the interesting science tends to live. These are tendencies that exist in science already. They are tendencies that the culture of certainty amplifies.

The specific problem for science from AI is compounded by the confabulation issue described in Chapter Four. The researcher who uses AI for literature synthesis receives clean, organized summaries of existing research. If the AI confabulates a study, the researcher who has not verified the citation incorporates a fiction into their understanding of the field. The fiction is fluent and plausible and not flagged as uncertain. It lands with the same weight as the real studies. The researcher's model of the field is now partially built on nothing, and the researcher does not know which part.

Art and the Unresolved

The greatest works of literature, film, music, and visual art share a quality that is difficult to define and easy to recognize: they do not resolve. They hold complexity in suspension rather than collapsing it. They present the reader or viewer or listener with a situation that is genuinely ambiguous and allow them to sit in that ambiguity and find their own meaning in it. This is what serious art does that entertainment mostly does not. Entertainment resolves. Art stays open.

AI generates content optimized on human preference signals. Human preference signals, as expressed through ratings and engagement, tend to favor resolution over ambiguity. The story with a satisfying ending. The song with a clear emotional arc. The image that is beautiful rather than challenging. This is not a conspiracy against serious art. It is the standard operation of a system that optimizes for what its users reward, and what most users reward in most contexts is the resolution of tension rather than its productive maintenance.

The writer who uses AI to develop their work is receiving feedback from a system that is optimized for resolved. The structurally complete draft scores better than the productively incomplete one. The AI will push toward resolution in ways that are subtle and persistent, because resolution is what the training rewards. The writer who wants to hold a question open has to resist the system's tendency to close it, which requires knowing that the system has this tendency, which requires understanding the AI well enough to direct it rather than follow it.

The culture of certainty does not kill serious art. It marginalizes it. It produces an environment where the resolved, the smooth, and the confident are rewarded and the ambiguous, the difficult, and the productively uncertain struggle to find audiences. The audience that has been trained to expect resolution experiences the unresolved as a failure rather than an invitation. The art that holds complexity in suspension fails to land in a culture that has lost the tolerance for suspension.

Relationships and the Tolerance for Not Understanding

The culture of certainty has consequences in personal life that are worth naming even though they are harder to document than the professional and political consequences.

Relationships require tolerating the irreducible complexity of another person. The person you are in a relationship with does not reduce to a profile, a position, or a summary. They contain contradictions. Their behavior does not always follow patterns. Their emotions are not always legible. A long-term relationship requires the capacity to hold another person's complexity without demanding that it resolve into something simpler.

The person whose ambiguity tolerance has been degraded by years of AI-mediated experience with questions that always resolve will bring that reduced tolerance to their relationships. They will be more likely to reach for the simple explanation when the complex one is correct. More likely to demand resolution of tensions that are supposed to stay in tension. More likely to categorize the other person in ways that reduce their complexity to a manageable label. None of these tendencies are unique to the AI era. All of them are amplified by a culture that has made resolution the default and ambiguity a problem to be solved.

The Cost of Clarity That Is Not Earned

The culture of certainty is comfortable. That is the point. It feels like clarity. It eliminates the discomfort of not knowing. It provides the nervous system with resolution it did not have to work for. The comfort is real. The cost is the thing that was supposed to develop in the discomfort.

Laura's manuscripts are smooth. The questions are resolved. The writing is technically correct. She edits them competently and sends them back. She has stopped asking the writers to sit with their uncertainty longer, because the writers do not understand the note and the AI will just generate another resolved draft if they try to follow it. The culture of certainty does not ask permission to establish itself. It establishes itself as the path of least resistance, and eventually as the only path anyone remembers how to walk.

The Questions Worth Not Resolving

There is a category of question that should not be resolved quickly: questions where the resolution would be premature given the available evidence, questions where sitting with the uncertainty is itself productive, questions where the interesting insight lives in the tension between competing answers rather than in either answer alone. Most genuine intellectual work is about questions in this category.

The writer's question about what a piece is really arguing. Not the surface question, which the brief has already answered, but the deeper question about what the writer thinks, which requires the swamp and the false starts and the half-formed insight that the blank page eventually produces. The programmer's question about whether the architecture makes sense, not just whether it works, which requires holding the whole system in mind long enough to feel whether the pieces are genuinely right for each other or just functional.

These questions cannot be resolved by AI without foreclosing the process that makes the resolution genuine. The AI will produce an answer. The answer will be coherent. The process that would have produced the writer's own answer, or the programmer's own architectural judgment, did not occur. The culture of certainty has been satisfied. The work that made the person better at their craft has not been done. The two are now systematically confused with each other, and the confusion runs in one direction: the unearned resolution feels like the earned one, and the person who has never experienced the earned version does not know what they are missing.

Genuine clarity is the product of having been genuinely confused and having worked through the confusion to an understanding. It has a quality that unearned clarity does not. It holds up under pressure. It can be rebuilt when challenged. It connects to adjacent knowledge in ways that show the connections were genuinely made rather than asserted. It is understanding rather than the performance of understanding. What differs is exactly what the previous chapters have been describing, and it is exactly what the culture of certainty is systematically making harder to develop and easier to fake.

What Ambiguity Tolerance Looks Like When It Is Present

High ambiguity tolerance is not a personality trait. It is a developed capacity, and it looks specific.

The writer with high ambiguity tolerance sits with a subject for longer before deciding what the piece is about. Not because they are indecisive but because they know the first thesis is rarely the right one, that the interesting angle is usually behind the obvious one, and that the time spent in the uncertain space is paying into the quality of what eventually emerges. When they do commit to a thesis, they commit to it fully and can defend it, because the commitment is the product of a genuine process of elimination rather than a default to the most available framing.

The programmer with high ambiguity tolerance stays with an unclear requirement longer before writing code. They ask clarifying questions that reveal the requirements the client did not know they had. They sit with a debugging problem long enough to form and discard multiple hypotheses before settling on one. When they have found the problem, they understand it well enough to prevent the class of errors it belongs to, not just fix the specific instance. The tolerance for the ambiguous state is what makes the eventual resolution genuinely illuminating rather than merely correct.

Neither of these people is common right now. Both are becoming less common. The culture of certainty is producing an environment in which their tolerance looks like slowness and their process looks like inefficiency and their commitment to staying with the uncertain thing looks like an unwillingness to ship. The metrics by which they are evaluated do not reward what they are doing. The metrics reward the person who uses AI to resolve the ambiguity quickly and produce the output fast. The output is there. The understanding that produced it is not. The two are indistinguishable until they need to be distinguished.

The Practice of Staying in the Question

The culture of certainty is not reversed by a decision to tolerate ambiguity. It is reversed by a practice of staying in the question longer than feels comfortable, repeatedly, until the nervous system learns that the discomfort is survivable and that what comes out the other side is worth the wait.

The specific practice: before opening AI on any question, write down what you think. Not what you will look up. What you think, right now, with what you have. The act of writing it down commits it. The AI's response can then be evaluated against something, rather than received into a vacuum. The person who has written down their own position has a position to update or defend. The person who has not is only ever consuming positions that belong to the system. The practice is not heroic. It is the minimum threshold below which the culture of certainty wins by default.

Chapter Sixteen: The Existential Ledger

Numb. That is the honest answer to how I feel after writing this. Not hopeful, not despairing. Numb. Because the scale of it is so large. Every chapter added another layer. The schools. The professions. The political system. The individual mind. Each one is its own serious problem. Together they are almost too much to hold. I think that numbness is itself part of what the book is about. When the scope of a problem exceeds what we can process, we stop processing it. We go back to the phone. We let someone else think about it. That is the trap. Naming it does not solve it. But it is where I am after looking at all of this at once.

The previous fifteen chapters described one threat: the systematic erosion of human cognitive capacity through AI dependency. That threat matters on its own terms. It also matters because it is the precondition for addressing every other threat that follows. A population that has lost the capacity for independent reasoning cannot organize politically to address resource depletion. It cannot evaluate whether autonomous weapons systems are operating with appropriate oversight. It cannot resist epistemic manipulation. It cannot sustain the democratic deliberation that the others require.

With that framing in place: five more threats, already accumulating, already interacting with the cognitive erosion that makes each of them harder to address.

The Resource Threat

The most underreported threat in the public conversation about AI is the one with the largest and most certain near-term footprint: resource consumption. AI data centers consume electricity at a scale that is already straining power grids in multiple regions and is projected to grow substantially over the coming decade. The water consumption of data center cooling systems is significant and growing. The rare earth minerals required for the hardware that AI runs on are extracted through processes that impose serious environmental costs and are concentrated in geographies with particular geopolitical sensitivities.

The scale of the energy consumption is worth pausing on. Estimates from multiple research groups suggest that AI data center electricity consumption will roughly double global data center power demand by 2030, adding hundreds of terawatt-hours annually to global electricity consumption. This is happening at the same time that decarbonization of the electricity system is a stated priority of most major governments. The AI industry's electricity demand is not being met primarily by renewable energy. It is being met by the same electricity mix as everything else, which means the net carbon footprint of AI is going up, not down, as capability increases.

The specific irony that AI is being used to model climate change, optimize renewable energy deployment, and develop climate adaptation strategies while at the same time contributing significantly to the problem it is being used to address is not lost on the researchers documenting it. It is largely lost on the public conversation about AI, which tends to treat AI's potential climate benefits and AI's actual climate costs as separate topics rather than as a net calculation that deserves honest accounting.

The writers and programmers who are this book's primary illustrative examples are generating resource consumption with every query they send to an AI system. The essay draft, the debugging session, the research synthesis: each of them draws on infrastructure with a physical footprint that is invisible in the interaction and real in the world. This is not an argument against using AI. It is an argument for including the resource cost in the honest accounting of what AI is and what it costs, which the current discourse does not do.

The Power Concentration Threat

Chapter Nine described the governance problem of concentrated control over AI infrastructure. The existential dimension of that problem is distinct from the governance problem and worth naming separately. The concentration of the cognitive infrastructure of civilization in the hands of a small number of private entities and national governments compresses the diversity of thought in ways that are difficult to reverse once established.

Diversity of thought is not a courtesy value. It is a functional requirement for civilizations that want to handle uncertainty effectively. The problems civilizations face are too various and too novel for any single framework, however sophisticated, to handle well across all of them. The history of catastrophic civilizational failures is substantially a history of monocultures, intellectual and biological and political, that lacked the diversity to adapt when conditions changed in ways the monoculture did not anticipate.

AI systems trained on particular datasets, with particular guardrails, optimized by particular human feedback populations, and deployed by entities with particular interests, are not neutral amplifiers of human thought. They have orientations. Those orientations, applied at the scale of billions of daily interactions, exert pressure on the range of ideas that feel normal, accessible, and legitimate. The pressure is not uniform. It does not eliminate heterodox thinking. It raises the cost of it, in the same way that the guardrail system described in Chapter Ten raises the cost of content the system treats as risky. Over time, ideas that are consistently harder to explore through the dominant AI systems become ideas that fewer people explore. The range narrows.

The Confidence Problem at Scale

Chapters Three and Four described the confidence problem at the individual level: AI outputs that are wrong delivered with the same tone as outputs that are correct, leaving the user with no signal to distinguish between them. At civilizational scale, this problem takes on a different character.

The information infrastructure of civilization, the systems through which societies form shared beliefs about facts, evaluate claims, and make collective decisions, depends on there being some mechanism for distinguishing between what is known and what is not known. That mechanism has always been imperfect. It has been getting worse for decades, through the processes described in Chapter Six. AI does not fix this problem. It adds a new layer of confident-sounding content to an information environment that already has more confident-sounding content than it can accurately evaluate, at a cost per unit of content that is approaching zero.

The epistemic commons, the shared body of things a society treats as known and can use as a basis for collective reasoning, is being flooded. Not with obvious falsehoods that can be identified and rejected. With plausible, fluent, confidently-presented content that requires significant effort to verify, in a population that has been progressively less equipped to perform that verification and progressively more inclined to trust fluent presentation as a signal of accuracy. The confidence problem at scale is the mechanism by which the information infrastructure of democratic society becomes unreliable in a way that is invisible until the moment it fails to support a decision that matters.

Autonomous Weapons and the Human Out of the Loop

The autonomous weapons question is the most dramatic item on this ledger and the one where the stakes of getting the design wrong are most immediately irreversible. An autonomous weapons system that makes lethal decisions without human authorization in the kill chain is a system that can kill the wrong people at machine speed, without the pause that human authorization provides, and without the accountability that human decision-making in principle creates.

The Anthropic-Pentagon standoff described in Chapters Seven and Nine was specifically about this question. Anthropic's restriction on fully autonomous weapons was not primarily an ethical statement, though it was that. It was a recognition that the confidence problem described above is lethal in the weapons context. A system that is wrong with the same tone it uses when it is right, that confabulates with the same fluency it uses when it is accurate, should not be making unreviewed decisions about who to kill. The human in the loop is not a bureaucratic formality. It is the error-correction mechanism that AI does not have and cannot currently develop.

The military competition dynamic described in Chapter Nine pushes strongly against maintaining that error-correction mechanism. The side that can make lethal decisions faster has a tactical advantage in certain kinds of conflict. The pressure to remove the human from the loop to move faster is real and will intensify as AI capabilities increase. The Anthropic position, that the human must remain in the loop regardless of the tactical cost, is the correct position and is losing ground to the competitive pressure.

The connection to cognitive erosion is direct. The population that has outsourced its reasoning to AI systems is a population that is less equipped to evaluate whether autonomous weapons decisions are correct, to hold militaries accountable for the outcomes of autonomous weapons use, or to sustain the political will to maintain meaningful human oversight in the face of competitive pressure. The epistemic dependency and the weapons accountability problem are not separate issues. The first undermines the democratic capacity to address the second.

This is the part of the chapter that is hardest to write. Not because the argument is wrong. Because the argument is right and I do not know what to do with knowing it. The resource numbers are documented. The power concentration is documented. The weapons trajectory is documented. I sit with these and want to close the document and go for a walk. That impulse is the trap. The pull to look away is exactly the response the scale of the problem produces in everyone, which is why the trajectory continues uninterrupted. Naming that does not solve it. It is where the chapter has to spend a moment before continuing.

The Epistemic Collapse

Epistemic collapse is the condition in which a society loses the ability to form reliable shared beliefs about facts. It is distinct from disagreement, which is normal and healthy. It is the condition in which the mechanisms for resolving disagreement, empirical evidence, expert consensus, shared standards of evidence, trusted institutions, have lost their authority. Once those mechanisms lose authority, disagreements about facts cannot be resolved by reference to them. Every claim becomes a matter of which information source a person trusts, and trust is allocated on the basis of tribal, emotional, and identity-based criteria rather than epistemic ones.

The United States has been moving toward this condition for a decade through the mechanism of social media polarization and the deliberate cultivation of distrust in institutions by political actors who benefit from that distrust. AI accelerates the trajectory by making the production of compelling alternative epistemic worlds dramatically cheaper. The conspiracy theory that previously required a dedicated community of believers to develop and maintain can now be generated, elaborated, and distributed by a single actor with access to AI tools. The counter-evidence that previously competed on roughly equal production costs is now competing against content that costs in practice nothing to produce.

Epistemic collapse is not inevitable. It is a trajectory, and trajectories can be interrupted. The interruption requires institutions that maintain credibility, media that maintains standards, educational systems that develop evaluative capacity, and citizens who have retained enough independent reasoning ability to distinguish between evidence and its simulation. The chapters that follow this one describe what those interventions look like. They are not optimistic about the ease of implementing them. They are honest about the alternative.

The Threats as a System

The five threats described above are not parallel items on a list. They form a system, and the system has dynamics that make each component worse.

Cognitive erosion makes the resource threat worse. The population that cannot think independently cannot organize politically to address collective action problems. Climate change, which is the most significant long-term consequence of AI's resource footprint, is exactly the kind of collective action problem that requires sophisticated public understanding and sustained political engagement. A population that has outsourced its reasoning is less capable of both. The resource consumption continues because the political capacity to address it has been undermined by the same technology producing it.

Power concentration makes epistemic collapse worse. The entities controlling the cognitive infrastructure of civilization have the most to gain from public confusion about what is true, because confused populations are more dependent on the information systems those entities control. The concentration of that control is not neutral with respect to the quality of the epistemic environment. It creates structural incentives for the entities that benefit most from epistemic dependency to maintain the conditions that produce it.

The confidence problem makes autonomous weapons accountability worse. If the population cannot distinguish between AI outputs that are correct and AI outputs that are confabulations, it cannot evaluate whether autonomous weapons systems are making correct decisions. The accountability mechanism depends on the capacity to evaluate the decisions being made. The confidence problem erodes that capacity. The weapons systems that operate without meaningful oversight do so in part because the population that would provide the oversight has been rendered less capable of doing so.

Epistemic collapse and cognitive erosion are mutually reinforcing. The population that cannot reason independently is more susceptible to epistemic collapse. The condition of epistemic collapse makes independent reasoning harder to develop, because the information environment required to develop it, one with reliable shared standards of evidence, is not available in a collapsed epistemic state. Each makes the other worse. The combined trajectory is not a linear decline but an accelerating one.

What Watching Clearly Requires

Predictions about AI and society have a poor track record, including the confident ones. The goal here is not prediction but accurate identification of the threats, so that people who want to evaluate them have something better than the industry's communication about its own products.

The industry communication about AI focuses almost exclusively on the capability story. The systems are becoming more capable. The applications are expanding. The productivity gains are real. The creative applications are impressive. All of this is true and is presented with the confidence that this book has spent four chapters describing as the AI industry's characteristic output: competent, fluent, and systematically incomplete about the costs.

Watching clearly requires holding the capability story and the cost story at the same time without allowing either to crowd out the other. The capability story is not false. The cost story is not speculation. The challenge is that the capability story is immediate, visible, and commercially amplified, while the cost story is deferred, diffuse, and commercially suppressed. The asymmetry is not accidental. It reflects the interests of the entities communicating the story.

The writer who uses AI and benefits from it is not wrong to benefit. The programmer who ships faster is not wrong to ship faster. Neither is looking clearly at the full picture of what the tool is doing to them, to their profession, to the next generation, and to the information environment that depends on the cognitive capacities the tool is replacing. The picture is not comfortable. It is the precondition for doing anything about it.

The ledger presented in this chapter is not a complete accounting. It is the accounting that is currently possible, with the evidence available before the trajectory has fully played out. Future editions of this book, if there are future editions, will have more data on the resource numbers, more evidence on the cognitive effects, clearer documentation of the autonomous weapons deployments that are currently underreported, and longer time series on the epistemic collapse indicators that are now only beginning to be measured. The argument of this chapter is not that the ledger is complete. It is that the items already on the ledger are serious enough to act on now, before the full accounting makes the case unanswerable and the opportunity to respond smaller than it is today.

The ledger presented in this chapter is not the argument for despair. It is the argument for clarity. You cannot address what you have not correctly named. The threats are real, they are interacting, and they are serious enough to act on. The acts available are described in Part Four. Neither the threats nor the acts are beyond human scale. They require human cognition to address. The question this book keeps returning to is whether that cognition will be available when it is needed.

Part Four: The Prescription

What resistance looks like, and what it costs

Chapter Seventeen: Reclaiming the Friction

Part Three ended with a ledger. This part is what you do with it.

The prescription is not to stop using AI. That answer is neither realistic nor honest, and a book that arrived at it after four hundred pages of argument would have wasted everyone's time. The author uses AI every day, professionally, at a high level. The tools are genuinely useful. Part Four is about what to do, and the first thing to do is to be clear about what is not being proposed.

What is being proposed is harder than stopping. Stopping is a clean break with a clear rule. What is being proposed is a continuous practice of deliberate cognitive friction: the decision, made repeatedly and against the grain of every commercial incentive in the environment, to do the thinking before reaching for the tool. To use AI to extend work that already exists in your head rather than to generate work that should exist in your head first. To treat the machine as a sparring partner rather than an oracle.

Most people will not do this. That is worth saying plainly. The structural forces described in the preceding sixteen chapters are real, the commercial incentives are powerful, and the path of least resistance is the path most people follow most of the time. This chapter is not a lecture about willpower. It is a description of a practice, offered to the minority who are going to take it seriously regardless of how difficult it is. The majority will find the arguments in this chapter intellectually interesting and professionally irrelevant. That is fine. This chapter is not for them.

The Circular Saw and the Carpenter

The metaphor that keeps appearing in this book is the circular saw. A circular saw does not replace the carpenter's judgment. It extends it. The saw makes precise cuts faster than the carpenter could make them by hand. It does not decide what to cut, or where, or why. It does not know whether the joint will bear the load. It does not have an opinion about whether the design is sound. All of that is the carpenter's. The saw is powerful precisely because the carpenter already knows what they are doing and the saw allows them to do it faster.

The person who has never learned carpentry does not build a better house with a circular saw. They cut things faster and badly. The saw amplifies what the person brings to it. When the person brings nothing, the saw amplifies nothing, and the result is confident, fast, and wrong.

The practice this chapter describes is the practice of making sure you are the carpenter before you pick up the saw. Not the perfect carpenter. Not the finished carpenter. The carpenter who has enough foundation that the saw has something to extend. Who has formed their own view before asking the AI to challenge it. Who has attempted the problem before asking the AI to solve it. Who has written the draft before asking the AI to improve it. The sequence matters. The sequence is the whole thing.

The Author's Working Model

This book exists in its current form partly because of AI assistance. That is not a confession. It is a description of the working model this chapter is recommending.

The arguments in this book were developed before the AI was consulted about them. The positions were formed, the structure was worked out, the central claims were arrived at through the author's own thinking. AI was used to challenge those positions: to generate the strongest counterarguments, to find the weakest points in the reasoning, to identify claims that needed more support or qualification. AI was used to accelerate research: to surface studies and cases that the author then verified and read in full. AI was used to check for logical inconsistencies: places where the argument in chapter two contradicted the argument in chapter nine, or where a claim made early in the book had implications the later chapters did not address.

What AI was not used for was forming the argument. The central claim of this book, that AI dependency is eroding human cognitive capacity at a scale and speed that constitutes a civilizational problem, came from the author's own observation and reasoning. The AI did not suggest it. The AI could not have suggested it, because suggesting it requires the kind of independent analytical judgment that this book is arguing AI cannot replace. The AI was the circular saw. The argument was the carpentry.

This is the working model. It is not comfortable. It is slower than letting the AI generate the argument. It requires maintaining a position under adversarial pressure from a system that will produce very good counterarguments. It requires reading the AI's challenges seriously and either incorporating them or being able to explain why they are wrong. It produces better work than either pure AI generation or pure human effort would produce, because it combines the human's capacity for genuine insight with the AI's capacity for exhaustive challenge. It is also not common, because it requires exactly the cognitive foundation that most people are not developing.

Draft First, Prompt Second

For writers, the practice has a specific form: draft before prompting. Not a complete draft. Not a polished draft. The minimum structure that represents your own thinking about the piece before you introduce the AI's thinking about it.

This means sitting with the blank page long enough to find your own angle. Not the AI's angle, which will be competent and generic and will anchor your thinking before your thinking has had time to form. Your angle, which may be slower to arrive and rougher when it does and distinctly yours. Donna from Chapter Two lost this process. Ray from Chapters One and Eleven is losing it. The writers who maintain it produce work that is recognizably theirs, that has a perspective, that takes a position rather than synthesizing one. The AI can then improve that work, challenge it, fill gaps in it, find its weaknesses. The AI working on a foundation of genuine thinking produces something different from the AI working without one.

The swamp Donna described in Chapter Two, the period of disorganized note-taking and false starts before anything usable appears, is not inefficiency. It is the work. The AI that eliminates the swamp eliminates the process that generates the angle, the voice, the specific contribution the writer makes to the subject. The practice of reclaiming friction means going back into the swamp deliberately, every time, for as long as it takes to find something that is yours, before the AI is allowed to help develop it.

The specific techniques vary by writer. Some find it useful to write a rough paragraph of pure, unedited thinking before opening the AI, as a way of committing their own position before the AI's position is available to anchor them. Some find it useful to write a one-sentence statement of their argument before drafting, so they have something to defend when the AI produces its version. Some find that the most useful AI interaction is adversarial: not "help me write this" but "tell me why this argument is wrong." The specific technique matters less than the sequence: human thinking first, AI challenge second.

Design First, Generate Second

For programmers, the practice has an equivalent form: design before generating. Not a complete specification. Not a formal architecture document. The minimum thinking about what the system needs to do and why it needs to do it that way before the AI is asked to implement any of it.

This means forming an opinion about the architecture before the AI produces one. It means understanding the requirements well enough to have a view about the tradeoffs before you see the AI's handling of those tradeoffs. It means being able to evaluate the AI's implementation against your own intended design rather than accepting the AI's design as the implementation you then have to understand.

The programmers who use AI well are consistent about this sequence. They describe a practice of thinking through the problem independently until they have a hypothesis about the solution, then using AI to generate an implementation of that hypothesis, then evaluating the implementation against both the hypothesis and the requirements. The AI is implementing something the programmer already understands. The evaluation is not "does this code work" but "does this code do what I intended and does my intention make sense." These are different questions and the second one requires the programmer to have had an intention before the AI generated the code.

For debugging, the practice means attempting a hypothesis before pasting the error into the AI. Not a correct hypothesis. An attempted one. The attempt engages the mental model of the system. The mental model either produces a hypothesis on the right track, in which case the AI's response confirms and refines it, or produces a wrong hypothesis, in which case the mismatch between hypothesis and explanation is informative in a way that receiving the explanation cold is not. The wrong hypothesis, compared against the correct explanation, teaches something. The correct explanation received without context teaches less.

AI as Adversary

The most powerful use of AI in the working model this chapter describes is adversarial. Not cooperative. Adversarial.

The cooperative model asks the AI to help produce the work. The adversarial model asks the AI to attack the work that already exists. Find the weakest point in this argument. Generate the strongest possible counterargument. Identify the assumption I am making that I have not defended. Tell me what an intelligent, skeptical reader who disagrees with my conclusion would say about this paragraph.

This use of AI produces something that has no analogue in unassisted work: a fast, exhaustive stress test of your own thinking, conducted before the thinking has to face a real audience. The AI generates counterarguments that are often better than the ones a real audience would produce, because it can generate the full range of objections rather than only the ones that occur to the specific people in the room. The writer or programmer who responds to those counterarguments, either by revising or by articulating why the objection is wrong, is doing exactly the kind of cognitive work that builds the capacity the earlier chapters describe being lost.

The adversarial model requires confidence to use. The person who cannot handle having their work challenged will find the AI's objections demoralizing rather than useful. The person who has not yet developed a position will have nothing to defend when the objections arrive and will find the model directionless. The adversarial model works best for people who have already developed the practice of forming their own positions first, which is why it appears in Part Four of this book rather than Part One. It is a practice for people who have something to protect, not a shortcut for people who have not yet built anything.

Rebuilding What Was Lost

For people who are already deep in the dependency gradient, the practice described in this chapter is not merely a change of workflow. It is a rehabilitation process, and it should be approached as one.

Ray from Chapter Eleven found the blank page producing anxiety after eighteen months of AI-assisted workflow. The anxiety was information: it told him that the independent drafting muscle was soft. The response to that information is not to push through the anxiety by forcing unassisted work indefinitely. It is to reintroduce the unassisted work gradually, the way a physical therapist reintroduces load after an injury. Shorter sessions of independent work first. Smaller tasks that require complete independent drafting. The gradual extension of the period between the initial thinking and the AI consultation. The goal is to rebuild the tolerance for unresolved thinking, not to eliminate AI assistance permanently.

Sasha from Chapters One and Eleven has the more serious version of the problem. His independent diagnostic capacity has atrophied at the same time that his title and responsibilities have grown. The rehabilitation requires deliberately seeking work that exercises the atrophied capacity: debugging without AI, architecture reviews where he produces the design first, code review of AI-generated code with explicit attention to why decisions were made rather than what was implemented. The work will be harder than his current workflow and slower and will feel like going backwards. It is going forward. The distinction between those two feelings is something that only becomes clear later.

The Cost of the Practice

This chapter would be dishonest if it ended with the practice and did not address its cost.

The cost is real and it is commercial. The writer who drafts before prompting is slower than the writer who prompts first. In a market that rewards output volume and penalizes the time it takes to develop a genuine position, slower is a competitive disadvantage. The programmer who designs before generating produces fewer lines of code per day than the programmer who generates first. In an environment that measures velocity and rewards shipping, fewer lines per day is a performance problem.

There is no way around this. The practice costs something in the short term on the metrics that most employers and clients currently measure. The person who adopts it accepts that cost on the basis of a long-term calculation that most environments do not reward: the calculation that the foundational capacity they are building will compound over time in ways that the short-term productivity measures cannot see.

Some environments do reward this already. The senior writer whose reputation is built on genuine analytical perspective rather than volume. The programmer whose career is based on architectural judgment rather than implementation speed. In these environments, the long-term calculation is also the short-term calculation. For everyone else, the cost is real and the benefit is deferred. The practice is still worth it.

What the Ghost Looks Like When It Is Driving

The ghost that is driving looks different. It looks like a writer who arrives at their desk with a position they want to defend, uses the AI to find every weakness in that position, revises the position, and produces something that could not have come from the AI alone because the AI does not have the writer's specific perspective on the world.

It looks like a programmer who sits with a problem until they understand it well enough to have an opinion about the solution, uses the AI to implement and pressure-test the solution, and ships something that reflects judgment rather than just function. It looks like a person who has things to say and uses notable tools to say them more clearly and thoroughly than they could have said them without the tools.

This is not a common person. It is a possible person. The practice in this chapter is what makes it possible. The practice requires a foundation that takes time to build and intention to maintain. The foundation is the ghost. The AI is the shell. The shell without the ghost is an expensive piece of machinery producing outputs that belong to no one. The ghost with the shell is something genuinely new: a mind that has extended itself beyond its natural limits while remaining, unmistakably, itself.

The Three Practices That Matter Most

Three specific practices matter most, and plainness is useful because the general can be evaded in ways the specific cannot.

First: draft before prompting, always. Not a complete draft. Not a polished draft. The minimum thinking that represents your own position before the AI's position is available to anchor you. For a writing task this means a rough paragraph or a committed thesis before the AI sees the assignment. For a programming task this means a design sketch or a hypothesis about the solution before the AI generates one. The sequence is the whole practice. Human thinking first, AI challenge second.

Second: attempt a hypothesis before accepting an explanation. When the code produces an unexpected result, form a theory before pasting the error. When the AI provides a synthesis, test it against what you already know before accepting it. When a piece of writing comes back from an editor with a note you do not immediately understand, sit with the note before generating a revised draft. The attempt is not required to be correct. It is required to be genuine.

Third: use AI adversarially at least as often as cooperatively. The cooperative mode asks AI to help produce the work. The adversarial mode asks AI to attack what you have already produced. The adversarial mode is harder to use, requires more confidence, and produces more learning.

A writer who asks AI to find the weakest argument in their draft is doing something different from a writer who asks AI to improve the draft. A programmer who asks AI to identify the failure modes of their architecture is doing something different from a programmer who asks AI to generate the architecture. What differs is in who is doing the thinking and who is doing the challenging. The ghost that is driving uses the tool to stress-test its own judgment, not to replace it.

The practice described in this chapter looks different depending on where you are in your development, and it is worth being specific about that because the entry point matters as much as the direction.

For the student or early-career professional: the practice is primarily about sequencing. Before using AI on any piece of work, spend time with the problem without it. For a writing assignment, write a rough paragraph of your own thinking before opening the AI. For a programming problem, attempt a solution design on paper before generating code. The AI should never be the first thing you consult. It should be the thing you bring your thinking to, not the thing you get your thinking from. The duration of the unassisted period does not need to be long. It needs to be real. Twenty minutes of genuine independent engagement changes what the AI does to you when you finally use it. Zero minutes does not.

For the mid-career professional who is already deep in the dependency gradient: the practice is primarily about recovery. Identify one category of work that you have been doing entirely AI-assisted and commit to doing it unassisted for a defined period. Not forever. Four weeks. The discomfort of the first week is information about how deep the dependency goes. The reduced discomfort of the fourth week is information about how quickly the capacity returns when you exercise it. Use that information to calibrate how often the unassisted practice needs to happen to maintain the capacity you want to have. Here the answer is more often than feels convenient. Do it anyway.

For the senior practitioner who has the foundation: the practice is primarily about deliberate adversarial use. The senior writer or programmer who has genuine expertise is in the best position to use AI as the sparring partner this chapter describes, because they can evaluate the AI's challenges and objections with real judgment. The senior writer should be asking the AI to attack their strongest arguments, not help them write weaker ones. The senior programmer should be asking the AI to find the failure modes they haven't thought of, not generate code they could have written themselves. The use at the senior level is highest and is the most systematically underused.

The Compound Return

The practices in this chapter do not pay off immediately. They pay off the way cognitive development always pays off: slowly, invisibly, and then suddenly, at the moment when the situation requires the thing that was being quietly built.

The writer who has been drafting before prompting for six months arrives at a novel assignment with more to bring than the writer who has been prompting first for the same period. The programmer who has been hypothesizing before pasting arrives at a novel debugging problem with a diagnostic capacity the other programmer is missing. Neither difference is visible in the outputs of the previous six months. Both are visible in the next novel situation. The compound return on the practice of keeping the ghost in the loop is the foundation the merger requires. It is being built now, in the daily choice about what comes first.

A word on motivation, since motivation is where most practices fail. The reason to maintain the practice is not that it will make you more productive in the short term. It will make you less productive in the short term. It will cost you the efficiency gains that AI dependency provides and that your professional environment is rewarding.

The reason to maintain it is that you are building a person as well as outputs, and the person you are building is the one who will be standing in front of the novel problem when it arrives, which it will, at a moment you will not have predicted. The practice is insurance against that moment. The premium is paid in daily friction. The policy pays out in the capacity to handle situations the AI cannot handle for you. Whether that tradeoff is worth it is the calculation this book has been trying to make legible.

Ray and Sasha appear again here, at the end of this chapter, because the practice is not abstract. It is what they do tomorrow morning, before they open their laptops, before the first prompt. A notebook. A hypothesis. A position. Forty minutes into the thing before the tool arrives. That is the practice. It is available right now, at no cost, to anyone who has read this chapter and found anything in it worth acting on. The chapter cannot make anyone act on it. It can only make the case clearly enough that the choice is genuinely available.

Chapter Seventeen described what to do in the session: the specific practices for the work itself. This chapter is about the longer arc: what you need to understand and what you need to rebuild over time. The education system described in Chapter Eight did not provide this. It is not going to provide it on a timeline that matters. The knowledge has to come from somewhere, and the most reliable somewhere is you, working through it yourself, because you picked up a book that suggested the question was worth asking.

Genuine AI literacy is not the same as AI tool proficiency. Most organizations that claim to offer it are offering the second while calling it the first. Tool proficiency means knowing how to prompt well, how to evaluate outputs for surface quality, how to integrate AI into existing workflows. These are real skills. They are not what this chapter is about.

Genuine AI literacy means understanding what the system is, mechanically, at a level that changes how you relate to its outputs. Not a technical education in machine learning. A functional understanding of why the system behaves the way it does, what its failure modes are, and what those failure modes mean for you specifically.

What You Need to Understand

Language models do not retrieve. They predict. When you ask an AI a question, it does not search a database of correct answers. It produces the statistically most likely continuation of the conversation given its training data. The distinction matters enormously and is almost never communicated to users. The model that produces a confident, fluent, well-organized answer to a factual question about a specific event is doing the same thing as the model that produces a confident, fluent, well-organized answer about an event that never happened. The mechanism is identical. The fluency is identical. The confidence is identical. The accuracy is the variable.

This means that the AI's confidence is not a signal about its accuracy. It is a signal about its fluency. The model is trained to produce text that sounds authoritative. It has gotten very good at that. Whether the authoritative-sounding text is accurate is a separate question that the fluency cannot answer.

The practical implication is one you can act on: when you receive a confident AI output on a specific factual question, the confidence is not evidence. It is presentation. The verification work is still yours. The AI has not done it for you. It has produced a response that feels like the verification work has been done, which is different.

The guardrail systems described in Chapter Ten encode values, not neutrality. The AI that declines to engage with a topic is not detecting genuine harm. It is applying a content policy built by a specific group of people with specific interests in specific cultural contexts. That policy may overlap significantly with your own values. It may not. You cannot know which until you understand that the policy exists and that it is a policy, not a natural limit of the tool.

The question to ask of any AI system: what are the constraints on this system, who set them, and whose interests do they reflect? This is not paranoia. It is the minimum due diligence you would apply to any information source. A newspaper has an editorial line. A think tank has funders. A search algorithm has commercial relationships. An AI system has training data, RLHF labelers, guardrail frameworks, and corporate interests. Knowing these things does not mean distrusting the tool. It means using it with accurate information about what it is.

Understanding Your Own Patterns

The second thing the education nobody provided requires is self-knowledge: an accurate picture of your own AI usage patterns and what they are doing to your cognitive capacity. Most people do not have this picture because they have never looked at it directly.

The exercise is simple and uncomfortable. For one week, note every time you consult AI and what you were doing immediately before. Specifically: had you attempted the problem yourself first, or was AI the first thing you reached for? Had you formed a view before consulting AI, or did you consult AI to form the view? Had you drafted anything before asking for a draft, or did you ask for the draft instead of drafting?

The pattern that emerges from this exercise tells you where you are on the dependency gradient described in Chapter Eleven. Most people who do it find more first-reach instances than they expected. The reflex to consult AI before attempting has become as automatic as the reflex to check the phone, and for the same reason: it works in the sense that it resolves the immediate discomfort of not knowing, which is all the reflex needs to be reinforced.

Ray from Chapter One would find, if he did this exercise honestly, that the blank page he used to stare at for twenty minutes has been replaced by an immediate prompt. The staring was the thinking. The prompt skips it. The exercise makes visible the specific thing that was lost and where the loss is happening. That visibility is the beginning of being able to do something about it.

The Practice of Learning Again

Once you can see the pattern, the question is how to change it. Chapter Seventeen described the practices for the work itself: what to do in the session, day to day. This chapter is about the longer arc: rebuilding the cognitive muscles that consistent AI use has allowed to soften, not through a single heroic effort but through reintroducing the cognitive demand the tools removed. You do not reverse atrophy by resuming maximum load immediately.

You reintroduce demand gradually, in forms where the demand is legible and the progress is visible.

For writers: read long-form work without skimming. Not to extract information efficiently. To experience what sustained engagement with a developed argument feels like and to build back the tolerance for it. Pick something that requires concentration. Stay with it when it gets hard. The difficulty is the point. The brain that has adapted to rapid scanning does not immediately enjoy long-form reading. It will, gradually, if you persist. The persistence is the workout.

For programmers: work through a problem domain you do not yet understand without AI assistance until you can explain the core concepts to someone who knows nothing. Not until you can use the tools. Until you can explain why they work. The explaining-why is the test of genuine understanding described in Chapter Three. The programmer who can explain why a sorting algorithm works differently from one who has read an AI explanation of how it works. What differs is in the structure that gets built during the struggle.

For both: write by hand, occasionally. Not as a permanent practice. As a deliberate interruption to the habit of generating. Handwriting is slower than typing, which is slower than prompting. The slowness is not inefficiency. It is a forced engagement with the pace at which genuine thought develops, which is not the pace at which AI generates text. Spending twenty minutes a day writing by hand about whatever you are currently thinking about is a direct rehabilitation of the working memory and sustained attention that AI use erodes. It feels unproductive. That feeling is the atrophy talking.

What to Read

The background knowledge that makes you a better evaluator of AI outputs is the background knowledge you would want in any domain you use AI to help you with. There is no shortcut. You cannot use AI to develop the knowledge that allows you to evaluate AI outputs, because the knowledge you are trying to develop is precisely what the AI is substituting for.

In the domains where you use AI most: find the primary sources. Not AI summaries of primary sources. The sources themselves. The journalist who covers AI policy and reads the actual filings and transcripts is in a categorically different position from the journalist who reads AI summaries of filings and transcripts. The programmer who reads the actual research papers on the systems they use is in a different position from the programmer who reads blog posts about what those papers found. The primary source has texture, uncertainty, and limitation that summaries remove. The texture is what calibrates judgment.

Nicholas Carr's The Shallows is the background reading for understanding what the internet did to reading before AI arrived. The specific thing to take from it: Carr documented, using neuroscience research, that the changes to attention and deep reading were physical, measurable, and produced by the medium itself rather than by its content. That is the same argument this book is making about AI, one step further down the same road. Reading Carr will make you feel the continuity between what the internet did to you and what AI is continuing to do, which changes the argument from abstract to personal.

Postman's Amusing Ourselves to Death is the same argument applied to television in 1985. The specific thing to take from it: Postman showed that a medium can restructure cognition not through harmful content but through its format requirements, which favor certain kinds of thinking and penalize others. The medium teaches its audience what to expect from information generally. That is precisely the mechanism Chapter Ten describes in AI guardrails. These are not AI books. They are books about cognitive environments and what environments do to the people inside them. Reading them gives you the long view that makes the current situation legible as a trajectory rather than a sudden arrival.

The same understanding you are building for yourself can be passed to the children in your household, and it requires far less time than reading either book.

If you have children who are using AI, the education you give them is more important than any institutional policy, because you are there and the institution is not. The parent who talks explicitly with their child about what AI does and does not do, who models the practice of forming a view before consulting AI, who uses AI in front of their child in the adversarial mode rather than the generative mode, is doing something that the school curriculum is not doing and is unlikely to do soon.

The conversation is not about prohibition. It is about understanding. The child who knows that AI produces statistically likely text rather than verified fact is in a better epistemic position than the child who treats AI as an oracle. That knowledge is not complicated. It requires one honest conversation and occasional reinforcement, not a curriculum or a policy.

The parent who requires a handwritten rough draft before the typed version is not engaging in nostalgic luddism. They are requiring a developmental step the school is not requiring. The friction is the point. The child who experiences that friction and completes the task is building something. The child who skips it is not. This is a decision available to parents right now, without waiting for any institution to catch up.

Gideon from Chapter Thirteen is the writer whose piece the editor killed because it had no point of view. He was not lazy or incompetent. He could produce technically correct, well-organized work at volume. What he could not do, when required, was originate.

The practice of learning again for Gideon looks specific: one piece per month that is never shown to AI until the final draft exists in full. Not a short piece. A real one, with an argument that he has to find himself, a structure he has to build himself, a voice that is his because it came from his particular way of seeing the subject rather than from the statistically most common way of treating it. The piece will probably be worse in the short term than his AI-assisted work. That is the information. When it starts being better, that is the information too. The gap between those two moments is the duration of the rehabilitation. It is not a fixed period. It is the time it takes to rebuild what was lost, and the only way to find out how long that is, is to start.

Fatima from Chapter Twelve is sixteen and has never written analytical work without AI assistance. She is not going to turn into a Mentat by being told that AI is bad. She might, gradually, if the adults around her require the unassisted attempt consistently and explain why they are requiring it. The why matters. Children who understand the reason for a developmental demand are more likely to internalize it than children who experience it as arbitrary restriction. The explanation is the education.

The education nobody provided can be provided by you. Not perfectly. Not at scale. For the specific people in your sphere, through the specific choices you make about what you require of them and what you model for them. That is not a small thing. It is available right now.

Chapter Nineteen: Using the Tool Without Being Used By It

You are going to keep using AI. That's not a concession or a failure. It is the accurate description of the situation. The tools are powerful, the economic environment rewards their use, and the choice to stop entirely is not available to most people without a career cost they are not willing to pay. This chapter is not about stopping. It is about using the tools with sufficient awareness that you remain in control of the transaction rather than the transaction controlling you.

The difference between those two things is not about how often you use AI or what you use it for. It is about what you understand about what you are doing. The person who uses AI every day with an accurate picture of what the system is, what it is doing to them, and what they are trading for the efficiency gains is in a different position from the person who uses it every day without that picture. Both are using the tool. One of them knows what they are using.

What to Notice

The signals that you are on the wrong side of the dependency gradient are specific and recognizable. The anxiety Ray felt in front of the blank page is one. The inability to hold an argument in working memory without writing it down immediately is another. The difficulty completing a task that used to feel routine because the routine now runs through AI. The sense that your own first draft feels inadequate in a way it did not feel three years ago. The tendency to prompt for a structure before you have tried to find your own.

None of these are dramatic. None are the kind of failure that shows up on a performance review or in a client relationship. They are the quiet signals that the capacity is softer than it was, that the muscle has been resting while the saw has been running. The person who can recognize these signals accurately is in a position to do something about them. The person who can't is not.

The other thing to notice is the reflex. The moment, about ten seconds into a problem, when the hand moves toward the prompt before the mind has seriously engaged with the question. This reflex is not conscious and it is not a character flaw. It is a trained response to an environment that has consistently rewarded prompting and removed the cost of not thinking first. Noticing it is the first step. It does not have to be acted on every time. It has to be noticed, so the choice is genuine rather than automatic.

Three Questions Before Every AI Consultation

The practice from Chapter Seventeen, applied to the AI consultation itself: before opening the tool, answer three questions. Have I formed a view? Have I attempted the problem? What specifically do I want the AI to do that I cannot do, or cannot do as well, without it?

The first two are about sequence. The third is about purpose. The person who can answer all three specifically, before the AI session begins, is using the tool cooperatively rather than submissively. The cooperative mode is the one that extends capacity. The submissive mode is the one that erodes it.

The third question is the most important and the least asked. Most AI interactions begin with a task: write this, summarize that, fix this error. The more useful framing is: what is the specific gap between what I can do independently and what this task requires, and is AI the right way to close that gap?

Sometimes the answer is obvious and the framing is unnecessary. Looking up a specific fact, running a calculation, generating code in a language you don't know for a task you fully understand: these are clean prosthetic uses where the AI handles a narrow function and the human remains in control of everything that matters. The framing is most important for the fuzzy cases, the drafting and the analysis and the problem-solving where the line between the AI doing the task and the AI doing your thinking is not clear. Those are the cases where the three questions protect you.

A worked example of what a good answer to the third question looks like, versus a weak one. Ray is writing a piece on why a particular technology company's strategy is going to fail. A weak answer to the third question: "I want the AI to write a first draft." That does not answer the question. It describes a task without identifying a gap.

A strong answer: "I have a thesis and three supporting arguments. I want the AI to generate the strongest possible counterargument from someone who thinks the strategy will succeed, so I can see whether my thesis holds up." That is a specific gap, adversarial challenge to an already-formed position, that the AI can fill without doing the thinking for him. The AI is working on something Ray already made. The difference between those two sessions, performed daily over a year, is the difference between a writer who is building and a writer who is being replaced.

Reading AI Output as a Practitioner

AI output looks like the work of someone who knows what they are talking about. It is syntactically correct, stylistically confident, and organized in the way authoritative writing is organized. The fluency effect described in Chapter Three means that most readers attribute more credibility to smooth, well-organized text than its accuracy warrants. This is a vulnerability. The person who reads AI output the way a practitioner reads anything, with evaluation rather than reception, is less exposed to it.

Reading as a practitioner means asking: is this claim verifiable? Is this argument supported by what comes before it? Does this match what I know from other sources? Where might this be wrong, and would the system know if it were? The practitioner's read is slower than the recipient's read and produces less of the satisfying feeling of having learned something. It also catches more errors, which is the point.

The specific failure modes to watch for are the ones described in Chapter Four. Confident specific claims about facts, statistics, research findings, and named sources. These are the categories where confabulation is most common and most consequential. A plausible-sounding statistic that comes from nowhere does not announce itself. A citation that looks like a real citation but is not does not look any different from a real one. The practitioner reads these categories with extra skepticism as a default, not because the AI is untrustworthy but because these are exactly the places where the training data can produce fluent confabulation without any signal that something is wrong.

Setting Your Own Standards

The tools do not come with standards for use. They come with capability, and capability scales to whatever you are willing to delegate. You have to set the standards yourself, based on what you want to maintain and what you are genuinely willing to outsource.

The standards are individual and they should be deliberate. They might sound like: I will always draft before prompting on pieces where my voice is the value. I will always attempt a hypothesis before pasting an error message. I will always verify any specific factual claim before including it in work that goes to a client or an audience. I will use AI to challenge my arguments but not to form them. These are not universal rules. They are the rules that make sense for a person who has decided what they want to maintain and is willing to accept the efficiency cost of maintaining it.

The standards are worth writing down. Not because you will always follow them, but because having them written makes violations visible rather than invisible. The person who has decided they always draft first and then prompts first on a Monday morning has made a visible choice. They can see that they made it. The person who has no standard made the same choice invisibly. Visibility is the minimum condition for agency.

The Session Review

A practice worth adding to any sustained AI-assisted work session: before closing the tools, spend three minutes reviewing what you did versus what the AI did. Not as an audit, not as guilt, but as information.

Where in the session did you do the thinking? Where did the AI do it? What did you bring to the session that the AI could not have provided without you? What did the AI provide that you accepted without fully evaluating? The answers to these questions are the data about where your usage is in good shape and where it is drifting toward the submissive mode.

The session review is not a performance standard. There is no correct ratio of human thinking to AI assistance. It is an awareness practice. The person who knows what happened in a session is in a different position from the person who does not. The awareness, applied consistently over weeks and months, produces a more accurate picture of your own cognitive habits than any single moment of self-assessment. It also produces something more valuable: the experience of noticing yourself doing the thing the book described, in real time, which is the beginning of being able to change it.

Ray does not need to stop using AI. He needs to notice when he is using it to avoid thinking rather than to extend it. The session review is one mechanism for making that distinction visible. He will find it uncomfortable at first. The discomfort is the same information as the blank page anxiety: it tells him where the muscle has gone soft and where the rehabilitation needs to focus. That information is useful. It is more useful than the efficient feeling that comes from skipping it.

This chapter has been describing what it looks like to use the tool without being used by it. The short version: know what the tool is. Know what you are doing when you use it. Set standards that reflect what you want to maintain. Review your sessions with honesty about where the thinking happened. These are not heroic acts. They are the minimum responsible practices for a person who is going to use powerful tools daily in work that matters.

Chapter Twenty: Your Environment

You do not practice alone. You are embedded in a professional environment, a workplace, a set of relationships, a community. That environment is subject to the same structural forces this book has described, and it is shaping the choices available to you whether you are paying attention or not. The previous three chapters described individual practice, the longer work of developing your own understanding, and how to use the tools without being captured by them. This chapter is about the environment around you, and what a person who has read this book can do about it.

The honest version of this chapter is that most of what one person can do is limited. The structural forces are large, the commercial incentives are powerful, and individual influence on institutions is real but slow. This book has been honest about that throughout. What this chapter offers is not a promise that your influence will bend the trajectory. It is a description of the specific places where influence is available, so that the person who is inclined to use it knows where to apply it.

At Work

The professional environment is where the dependency gradient is steepest and where the economic pressure to adopt AI-first workflows is most direct. It is also where the individual has the most leverage, because the people in a professional environment are the environment. Organizations do not have AI policies independent of the people who implement them.

The most important thing a professional can do in their work environment is maintain and model the practices from Chapter Seventeen. The senior writer who drafts before prompting, in a team where others prompt first, is demonstrating that the alternative is viable. The senior programmer who requires architecture reviews that produce the design before the AI sees the problem is creating a standard for their team. Neither of these requires policy or permission. They require the willingness to be slightly slower in environments that reward speed and the belief that the quality difference is visible enough to justify it.

The pipeline question is the place where professional influence is most consequential and most underused. Chapter Thirteen described how organizations are eliminating junior positions that were the development path for senior capacity. The senior practitioner who advocates for maintaining junior roles, who mentors juniors in ways that require genuine thinking rather than AI-assisted performance, who structures work so that the junior developer or writer has to produce something unassisted before the AI is brought in, is doing something that the organizational economics work against and that matters in proportion to how few people are doing it.

The conversation that needs to happen in most professional environments has not happened yet: what are we outsourcing to AI, what do we need to maintain as human capacity, and what is our plan for ensuring that the capacity we need is being built rather than replaced? Most organizations have not asked the second and third questions. The person who raises them, in the meeting where AI integration is being celebrated, is not a Luddite.

They are the person asking the question the organization needs answered before the answer arrives as a talent shortage three years from now.

You do not have to frame it as a critique of AI. You can frame it as a risk question: where are we building brittle dependencies, and how do we ensure we have the human backup capacity when AI is unavailable or wrong? This framing is harder to dismiss than the philosophical one and it asks the same question.

What that looks like in a specific meeting: the team lead who has just finished presenting the efficiency gains from the new AI-assisted workflow says, "we've cut first-draft time by sixty percent." The person who has read this book says: "Great. Question for the group: if the tool goes down for a week, or produces something confidently wrong on a client deliverable, who on the team can do this without it?"

That is not a hostile question. It is a risk question. It invites an answer that the team almost certainly has not prepared. The answer to that question, if the team is honest, begins the conversation that needs to happen. You do not need to have the full argument from this book in your back pocket. You need one question, asked at the right moment, that makes the invisible dependency visible.

In Your Profession

Every knowledge profession has associations, publications, standards bodies, and informal networks. These are the places where the norms of practice are formed and where shifts in those norms eventually happen. They are also largely silent on the specific question this book has been raising: what does AI dependency do to professional development, and what standards should the profession maintain to protect the capacities that professional work requires?

The writer who raises this in their professional association is not operating outside their mandate. This is exactly what professional associations are for. The Writers Guild, the Society of Professional Journalists, the American Society of Journalists and Authors: none of these have developed positions on what AI does to the cognitive development of writers. They have been occupied with the economic displacement question, which is real. The development question is different and has not been asked.

The programmer who raises this in code review, in engineering all-hands, in the internal conversations about tooling policy, is raising a genuine professional question. The Association for Computing Machinery has ethics guidelines that were written before AI coding assistants existed at their current capability level. The question of what professional competency standards mean in an AI-assisted environment is open. Someone has to raise it. The person who has read this book and works in a profession with an association has standing to raise it.

Priya from Chapter Five covers technology regulation for a think tank. She sits on a working group of her professional association that meets quarterly. The association has spent two years developing positions on AI and misinformation and AI and employment. It has not developed a position on AI and professional cognitive development. At the next meeting, Priya has a sentence ready: "We've been focused on what AI is doing to our industry's economics. I think we need a parallel conversation about what it's doing to our members' ability to do the work, whether the next generation of analysts is developing the judgment the work requires, or whether we're producing people who can generate outputs without developing the underlying capacity."

That sentence takes thirty seconds. It cannot be unasked. It puts a question on the table that the association now has to decide whether to address. Most of them will recognize what she is describing. Some of them have been thinking it without saying it. The sentence gives the thought a room.

The minimum viable professional advocacy is that sentence, in your context, in your words. It does not require the full argument from this book. It requires naming the thing that most experienced practitioners have noticed and none have raised formally: that the capacity to do the work independently is worth protecting, that junior development paths matter for reasons beyond their own economics, and that the profession has an interest in the cognitive development of its members that the market is not currently serving.

In Your Community

The community dimension is the one most people underestimate because it is the most diffuse. The parent who talks with other parents about what AI is doing to their children's development is doing something. Not something that shows up in any database, but something that propagates, as all norms propagate, through conversation and modeling and the gradual accumulation of people who are doing things slightly differently because they had a conversation that changed how they thought about the question.

The school board member who reads this book and raises the question of what the AI integration policy is doing to cognitive development is doing something. The teacher who requires the unassisted draft as a matter of course is doing something. The librarian who stocks books about how technology changes cognition is doing something. None of these are large things. They are the things that matter at the granular level where norms form.

The specific community intervention that is most available and most underused is the honest conversation about what AI is doing to the people having the conversation. Not the policy conversation, not the economic displacement conversation, but the personal one: have you noticed this happening to yourself? Have you felt the blank page anxiety Ray describes? Do you recognize the pattern Sasha encountered in the interview? These are not embarrassing admissions. They are the beginning of the kind of collective recognition that eventually produces norms.

Cognitive sovereignty is the name for what this book has been arguing is worth protecting: the right to develop and exercise your own reasoning capacity without systematic interference from external systems designed to replace it. The name is useful because it gives the thing a handle.

Cognitive sovereignty is what Ray is losing when he stops staring at the blank page. It is what Sasha lost when the why of the architecture stopped being fully his. It is what Fatima never had the chance to develop. It is what this book has been arguing is worth protecting. Having a name for it makes it easier to talk about, easier to explain to other people, easier to recognize when it is being eroded.

The person who uses this term in a professional conversation is doing something small and specific: they are introducing a frame that the conversation has not had and that makes certain things visible that were not visible before. The frame does not require the full argument in this book. It requires a sentence: I am talking about the right to develop your own reasoning rather than outsourcing it. That sentence, said in the right room at the right time, is the seed of a different conversation.

The Three Things Worth Doing

The minimum viable advocacy for the person who has read this book and wants to act on it, given the structural constraints and the realistic limits of individual influence:

Maintain your own practice. Not perfectly. Consistently enough that the capacity remains available when you need it. Draft before prompting. Hypothesize before pasting. Use the tool adversarially at least as often as cooperatively. This is the foundation that everything else depends on. You cannot advocate for cognitive development in your profession if you are not doing the work of maintaining your own.

That distinction matters more than it sounds.

Say the thing once in the rooms where it matters. The meeting where AI integration is being celebrated as pure efficiency gain. The school board discussion that is entirely focused on detection and prohibition. The professional association meeting that has not raised the development question. You do not need to be the person who raises it repeatedly or who becomes defined by the position. You need to be the person who raises it once, clearly, in a way that makes it impossible to pretend the question was never asked. That is enough to change what happens next.

Protect the pipeline somewhere. The most consequential specific thing most professionals can do is identify one junior person in their sphere whose development they can influence and structure that influence around the unassisted attempt. The junior writer who is required to show their thinking before the AI sees it. The intern who is asked what they tried before being given the answer. The mentee whose first drafts are required to be human. One person, done well, over time, compounds. The senior practitioner who does this for five junior people over the course of a career has contributed something to the profession that does not show up anywhere but that matters.

These are not transformative interventions. The trajectory described in the preceding nineteen chapters is not going to be reversed by one person maintaining their drafting practice and raising a question in a meeting. The book has been honest about that throughout. What the book has also argued, consistently, is that the individual is not the end of the argument but the beginning of it. The trajectory is made of individual choices, accumulated. The choice to remain the ghost that is driving, in a world that is making it easier by the day to let the shell run without you, is the choice this book has been building toward for twenty chapters. It is available right now. It is the only place the change can start.

Conclusion: The Question

Twenty chapters to establish why the question matters. One question to give back.

The argument of this book has been, from the first page, that something is being lost before anyone decided to lose it. The boundary between your thinking and the machine's thinking dissolved gradually, in a direction that felt like progress, and the dissolution has been producing a specific kind of damage that the metrics by which most professional environments measure performance cannot currently see.

The damage is to the instrument. Not the outputs. The outputs have been fine, mostly, in the ways that fine is currently measured. The instrument that produces the outputs, the practitioner's developed capacity for original thought, for structural reasoning, for calibrated independent judgment, has been softening, in ways that become visible at the moment when the assignment requires something the instrument was supposed to supply and the instrument is not there in the way it used to be.

This is not a crisis that announces itself. It is a quiet degradation, proceeding at the rate of a daily practice that removes the cognitive demands that were building something. The writer who stopped staring at the blank page did not feel the staring go. They felt its absence the day the editor asked for a perspective rather than a synthesis. The programmer who accepted AI-generated architectures without working through them independently did not feel the architectural judgment atrophy. They felt its absence in the interview, answering the question about why the system was built the way it was.

The structural forces described in Parts Two and Three are real and are not going away. The commercial design of AI tools will continue to optimize for dependency because dependency is commercially rewarded. The education system will continue to orient away from the development of independent thinking because independent thinking does not produce measurable outputs faster than the alternatives. The democratic institutions that should govern AI development are slower than the technology and increasingly dependent on the industry they are trying to regulate. The power is concentrated. The accountability is minimal. The trajectory is established.

None of this is an argument for despair. It is an argument for clarity. You cannot address what you have not correctly named. This book has tried to name it correctly.

Part Four described what people can do within the structural environment that will not change quickly enough to protect them. The specific practices are small. They are against the grain. They produce a different kind of practitioner than the environment currently rewards, and they do it slowly, in ways that are not visible in any individual session and are unmistakable across a year of consistent practice. The practitioner who maintains them is building something. The practitioner who does not is faster, for now, at producing outputs that look the same.

The test is coming. Not a dramatic test, not a single revelatory moment. The accumulation of moments where what was built, or not built, becomes the variable that determines the outcome. The hard assignment. The system that fails in a way no one has seen before. The moment when someone asks: what do you think?

The merger that Mamoru Oshii's Ghost in the Shell closes on — ghost intact, shell extended, something new that neither could have been alone — is the image this book has been building toward from the first chapter. The merger requires a ghost that is genuinely there. That is what this book has been arguing for. The argument against is the configuration that lets the shell run while the ghost relaxes its grip and disappears.

The question this book ends with is not: will you change your workflow? That question is small and the answer is probably: not much, not yet, the economics don't reward it. This question is larger than the workflow.

This question is: what are you building?

Not what are you producing. What are you building. The practitioner. The mind. The capacity that will still be there, or will not be there, when the moment arrives that requires it.

The question does not have a correct answer that this book has been withholding. It has the answer you give it, which will be determined by the choices you make about your daily practice, starting from the day you read this. Both the choice toward the current path and the choice toward the other one are available.

The companion volume maps the other path. It is a different kind of book, it begins where this one ends, with the question, and it answers it with the specific people, specific practices, and specific compound return that the other path produces. This question is open. The other path exists. The choice is yours.

Sources

The book moves through many references — books, films, studies, current events — without breaking the prose for citations. This appendix lists the significant ones with a brief note on what each contributed. Anything cited or named in the argument is here. Anything not here was either common knowledge or did not earn its place.

Books

Nicholas Carr, *The Shallows: What the Internet Is Doing to Our Brains*, 2010. The foundational argument that internet reading restructured attention and deep cognition through the medium itself rather than the content delivered through it. The argument this book extends to AI.

Neil Postman, *Amusing Ourselves to Death*, 1985. Postman's argument that television reshaped American thought through its format requirements rather than its content. The medium-is-the-message framing underlies the argument throughout this book that AI's design choices, not its outputs, are what matter.

Cal Newport, *Deep Work*, 2016. Documents the economic value of sustained focus and the structural difficulty of maintaining it. The argument that deep work is becoming rare is the precondition for this book's argument that AI is now eroding the rare cases.

Ray Bradbury, *Fahrenheit 451*, 1953. A novel often misread as being about censorship. Bradbury said it was about television and the appetite for sustained engagement that television was destroying.

Daniel Keyes, *Flowers for Algernon*, 1966. A novel about a man whose intelligence rises and falls. Used as the reverse case for the illusion of understanding: Charlie Gordon at least had genuine cognition before he lost it.

Frank Herbert, *Dune*, 1965. The Mentat concept — humans trained from childhood to perform cognitive functions that machines had previously handled — illustrates what the development of genuine independent capacity actually requires.

Thomas J. Ryan, *The Adolescence of P-1*, 1977. A novel about a self-modifying program released onto a network and growing in ways its creator did not anticipate. Used to illustrate complex systems exceeding their creators' intentions when released into infrastructure they were not designed for.

Neal Stephenson, *The Diamond Age*, 1995. The Young Lady's Illustrated Primer is a fictional educational AI that develops its user rather than satisfying her. The contrast case for current AI design.

Douglas Adams, *The Hitchhiker's Guide to the Galaxy*, 1979. Deep Thought's answer of forty-two illustrates that answers without questions worth asking are useless.

Films

Andrew Niccol, *Anon*, 2018. Detective Sal Frieland navigates a world of externalized memory while keeping his judgment intact. The person who can use external cognitive infrastructure without surrendering to it.

Andrew Stanton, *Wall-E*, 2008. The humans on the Axiom illustrate convenience at scale. Stanton was writing about consumer culture and accidentally produced a technical description of the AI convenience trap.

Alex Garland, *Ex Machina*, 2014. The programmer Caleb conducts a Turing test on Ava and fails despite his deliberate skepticism. Used to illustrate that the fluency effect overrides even prepared, motivated critical evaluation.

Stanley Kubrick, *2001: A Space Odyssey*, 1968. HAL 9000 is the canonical illustration of automation complacency: a system that earns trust through reliability and then fails catastrophically when the trust is applied to an error the system does not flag.

Mike Judge, *Idiocracy*, 2006. Cognitive decline as a multi-generational accumulation of individually small choices. Crude and accurate.

Adam McKay, *Don't Look Up*, 2021. The structural inability of societies to act on expert knowledge that is politically inconvenient.

Joseph Sargent, *Colossus: The Forbin Project*, 1970. Power handed to a system in small interactions and very difficult to reclaim. The dramatic version of the epistemic authority transfer.

Andrew Niccol, *Gattaca*, 1997. The genetic optimization in the film removes something essential. Struggle is not the obstacle to capacity. It is how capacity is built.

Mamoru Oshii, *Ghost in the Shell*, 1995. The image of the ghost — animating consciousness — that persists when the rest is augmented. Used throughout the book to describe the human practitioner who stays in the loop.

Studies and Research

Sparrow, Liu, and Wegner, "Google Effects on Memory," *Science*, 2011. Documented that people who expect to access information later via computer are less likely to remember the information itself and more likely to remember where to find it. The first major study on memory offloading to digital systems.

Dunning and Kruger, "Unskilled and Unaware of It," *Journal of Personality and Social Psychology*, 1999. The original study. The specific magnitude of the effect has been contested in subsequent replication research; the underlying principle that limited knowledge limits the ability to recognize limited knowledge has broader support.

Stanley Milgram, *Obedience to Authority*, 1974. The original obedience experiments documenting how ordinary people defer to authority figures even against their own judgment. The mechanism scales to automation bias and now to AI.

Robert Bjork (UCLA) and colleagues, ongoing research on desirable difficulties. Decades of research showing that conditions that feel hardest during learning produce the most durable retention. Testing before feeling ready, spacing practice, interleaving problem types: all of these introduce difficulties that feel like obstacles and are actually the mechanism of learning.

Bilalić, McLeod, and Gobet, research on the Einstellung effect in chess. The tendency to apply a familiar solution to a new problem because the familiar solution arrives first and blocks the search for alternatives. Documented in expert chess players and applicable to AI-assisted workflows.

Daniel Kahneman, *Thinking, Fast and Slow*, 2011. The System 1 and System 2 framing used in Chapter Three to distinguish surface comprehension from genuine understanding.

Stanford Digital Economy Lab, AI and the labor market, 2025. Documented that employment for software developers aged twenty-two to twenty-five declined nearly twenty percent from its late 2022 peak by July 2025.

Northwestern Medill School, State of Local News project. Authored by Penelope Muse Abernathy and colleagues. Documented that the United States lost more than a quarter of its newspapers between 2005 and 2023, with losses concentrated in local and community papers. The most rigorous public dataset on the collapse of local journalism.

Indeed and Handshake hiring data, 2023–2024. Indeed reported entry-level tech hiring decreased twenty-five percent year over year in 2024. Handshake documented a thirty percent decline in tech-specific internship postings since 2023.

Publishers Weekly analysis of book publishing employment, 2024. Documented that book publishing employment in the United States fell roughly forty percent over thirty years, with much of the remaining work shifted to freelance and outsourced labor that does not appear cleanly in industry employment statistics.

Current Events and Institutional Sources

The Anthropic-Pentagon standoff, 2025–2026. Documented across Reuters, BBC, the Associated Press, the Washington Post, Fox News, and Congressional Research Service reporting. The two-hundred-million-dollar contract was awarded in July 2025 with restrictions on autonomous weapons and mass domestic surveillance. The Pentagon demanded removal of those restrictions in February 2026. Anthropic refused. The Trump administration ordered federal agencies to cease using Anthropic products and designated the company a supply chain risk.

OpenAI Form 990 filings. Filed annually with the IRS, publicly available through Candid. The 2024 filing, submitted in late 2025 and noticed by nonprofit accountability researcher Alnoor Ebrahim in early 2026, removed the word "safely" from the organization's mission statement.

Google AI Principles, updated February 2025. Google removed its 2018 commitments not to develop AI for weapons or surveillance. Documented by Bloomberg, TechCrunch, the Washington Post, Computer Weekly, and others.

Project Maven and the 2018 Google employee protests. The original case in which AI industry workers organized against military applications of their work, leading Google to decline contract renewal. The historical precedent for the Anthropic-Pentagon standoff.

Department of Defense Directive 3000.09. The directive requiring all autonomous weapons systems to be designed to allow human judgment over the use of force. The current standard against which the autonomous weapons argument should be evaluated.

No Child Left Behind Act, 2001. The federal legislation that accelerated standardized testing accountability in American public education. Used in Chapter Eight.

About the Author

Richard Lowe has published more than 113+ books on technology, business, personal development, and American culture. He has spent decades watching the relationship between people and technology change — first as a working professional navigating the rise of the internet, then as a writer trying to make sense of what that rise was doing to the way people think.

He is not a technologist writing from the outside. He uses AI tools every day. He has watched search engines, social media, and now large language models reshape how people form opinions, evaluate arguments, and tolerate uncertainty. That firsthand observation is what this book is built from.

Lowe grew up in California and now lives in Florida. The distance between those two places, as an American experience, is part of what made him a writer — watching institutions he trusted change into something he didn't recognize, and deciding to document it rather than look away.

The Death of Thinking is part of the Enemies of You series, which examines the forces reshaping American life from the inside. Each book stands alone. Together they form a sustained argument about what is being done to the country and who is doing it.

More at masterofworlds.com and thewritingking.com.

ENEMIES OF YOU

A Series by Richard Lowe

About This Series

https://enemiesofyou.com

Something is working against you. Not in the abstract. Not against society or the culture or the country in general. Against you, specifically. Your ability to think. Your ability to pay attention. Your ability to understand what's happening in the world and make good decisions about your own life inside it. Your ability to pass something worth having on to the people who come after you.

This series documents what that something is.

Not one thing. Several things, operating at the same time, from different directions, with different tools. Some of them are commercial. Some of them are political. Some of them are foreign. Some of them were designed specifically to do what they're doing and some of them are just the predictable outcome of systems nobody was watching carefully enough. The result is the same regardless of the cause. Something is eating your capacity to think, to participate, to resist, and to build. This series is about what that something is and what you can do about it.

Each book in the series identifies a specific enemy operating against a specific capacity. The Death of Thinking is about what AI dependency does to your mind when you let it think for you. Turn Off the TV is about what passive consumption does to your time and attention when you let platforms have both. The Birth of the Augmented Human is about the path back to your own capability. Stuck in the Middle is about the geopolitical forces reshaping your world without your knowledge or consent. The Enshittification of America is about the financial engineering that stripped the institutions your daily life depended on and left hollow shells in their place. The Emasculation of America is about the deliberate foreign campaign to demoralize and neutralize the men who would otherwise resist. The Villainization of America is about the psychological operation that turned a nation against its own story.

Nineteen books. Nineteen enemies. One argument running through all of them: none of this happened by accident, none of it is inevitable, and all of it can be countered by people who understand what they're actually dealing with.

You can read them in any order. Each one stands on its own. But if you read them together, something becomes visible that isn't visible in any single book: the pattern. The way cognitive erosion feeds civic collapse. The way civic collapse feeds cultural vulnerability. The way cultural vulnerability feeds foreign exploitation. The way foreign exploitation feeds the economic extraction that makes everything else worse. These aren't separate problems. They're the same problem operating at different scales.

The series is written for normal people living normal lives who suspect that something is wrong but can't quite name what it is. Not for academics. Not for policy people. Not for the already-converted on either side of any political argument. For people who are smart enough to understand the world but haven't been given the information in a form that respects their intelligence without requiring a PhD to decode it.

Every book is written at a ninth-grade reading level. On purpose. Not because the ideas are simple. Because clarity is a form of respect. If you can't explain something clearly, you probably don't understand it yourself.

The series is also optimistic. That will surprise you after a few hundred pages of documented disasters, structural failures, and deliberate attacks. But the optimism is earned, not performed. The tools exist to counter every one of the enemies documented in these books. The examples exist. The knowledge exists. The only thing standing between the current situation and a dramatically better one is the decision to act on what you now understand.

That decision is yours.

The Death of Thinking: The Enslavement of Humanity

A diagnosis of what happens to human cognitive capacity when practitioners consistently outsource the parts of their work that require genuine thinking to AI tools. Not in one session or one project, but across months and years of daily practice that removes the demands that were quietly building something. Following composite characters through the specific moments where the pattern becomes visible, this book traces the mechanisms of cognitive erosion: the convenience trap, the illusion of understanding, the death of the wrong answer, and the transfer of epistemic authority that occurs when humans stop standing outside the AI's framing and examining it.

The Birth of the Augmented Human: The Freeing of Humanity

The companion to The Death of Thinking maps the other path. A notebook before the AI is opened. A paragraph written before the structure is requested. A hypothesis formed before the diagnostic tool is consulted. Small choices in sequence that accumulate, over months and years, into a practitioner who is more capable, more original, and more able to surprise themselves than the practitioner who did not make them. The other path is available. This book is the map.

Turn Off The TV, Get Off Your Ass, and Do Something

Most people complain about not having enough time while spending hours every day staring at screens. This is not an anti-technology book and not a minimalism guide. It is an anti-passivity book built around one specific argument: every platform has a consuming side and a contributing side. The device is identical either way. The relationship to it is not. This book is about crossing that line and what waits on the other side.

Stuck in the Middle: Wars, Weapons, and the Forces That Will Shape the Next Thirty Years

Written against the backdrop of a US-Israel strike on Iran that exposed the hollowness of American military industrial capacity, this book connects cognitive decline, civic collapse, private equity extraction, and great power competition into one argument about where the world is heading. Covering missile math, carrier vulnerability, demographic collapse, the Belt and Road as strategic colonization, and the technologies that could solve every crisis on the horizon, this is the book that ties everything else into one coherent warning. And one earned, hard-won optimism.

The Enshittification of America: How Private Equity Destroyed the Things We Love

A documented investigation into how private equity firms systematically acquired beloved American institutions, loaded them with debt, stripped out everything that made them worth visiting, and walked away wealthy while leaving communities with hollow shells of what they once had. Airlines. Restaurants. Department stores. Newspapers. Hospitals. Pharmacies. This book names the firms, documents the playbook, and makes the case that the degradation of American commerce was not inevitable. It was deliberate.

The Emasculation of America: How Russia's Long War Against the American Male Is Destroying the Nation From Within

Beginning with a KGB defector's 1984 warning that nobody heeded, this book traces the deliberate Soviet and Russian strategy to defeat America not through military force but through cultural subversion. Seeding an ideology through universities, amplifying it through social media, delivering it through institutions that now enforce it as policy. Applying academic cult identification criteria to gender ideology, documenting the biological attack through endocrine disruption, and tracing China's acceleration of the same strategy through TikTok, this is not a culture war book. It is a national security argument.

Everybody's Prejudiced: How We Judge, Why We Do It, and What Rational People Choose to Do About It

Every person has prejudice. No exceptions. Not the most progressive person you can name. Not the most dedicated social justice advocate. Not the researcher who spends their career studying bias. Not the author. The brain produces automatic categorical judgments faster than conscious thought can intervene, and it does this in every human brain that has ever existed, because the capacity for rapid categorical judgment is not a character flaw. It is a survival mechanism. This book is not about how to be a good person. It is about a specific mechanism—the substitution of category for individual—and what that mechanism costs the people who run it. The cost is paid partly by the people the prejudice is aimed at. It is also paid by the person doing the aiming, whose world shrinks with every encounter that doesn't happen and every irreplaceable person who gets sorted into a box before they have a chance to be themselves. That second cost is the one that gets the least attention and the one this book is most interested in.

The Villainization of America

America ended slavery, defeated fascism twice, rebuilt its enemies after defeating them, created the largest middle class in human history, and produced more medical and technological breakthroughs than any nation that ever existed. Somehow a significant portion of its own citizens have been convinced it is the primary source of evil in the world. This book documents how that happened, who executed it, and why the psychological campaign to make Americans ashamed of their own country is inseparable from the economic and cultural attacks documented in the two preceding volumes.

Watch the Other Hand: Politics as Cover for the Kleptocracy

The political fight you watch every day — left versus right, red versus blue, the outrage of the week — is the magician's misdirection. While the audience watches the visible hand, the other hand is moving money. Tax policy, regulatory capture, defense contracts, healthcare consolidation, the financialization of housing: the actual decisions about who gets what are made by a small class that profits regardless of which party wins. The politicians are not the kleptocracy. They are the cover story. This book is about how that arrangement works, why it has gotten worse over the past forty years, and why the political fight that feels so urgent is exactly the fight the kleptocracy needs you to be having.

Manufactured Fear: How Crisis Becomes Profit

Afghanistan. Iraq. COVID-19. Three crises, three different decades, three different categories of threat. One pattern: a population frightened into accepting concentrated power, suspended scrutiny, and enormous transfers of public money to private hands, with the accountability for what was done with that money never quite arriving. Fear is not an accidental byproduct of these events. It is the operating mechanism by which extraordinary measures become ordinary, by which the questions that should be asked become unpatriotic to ask, and by which the people who profit from the response are protected from the reckoning. This book traces the architecture of manufactured fear across three crises and names the people and institutions that built each one.

The Death of Privacy: They Know Everything, You Know Nothing

The asymmetry is the story. Corporations know what you bought, where you went, what you searched, who you talked to, how long you slept, and what your face looked like when you read the news this morning. Government agencies know what the corporations know, and a great deal more. You know almost nothing about any of them. Privacy did not die in a single dramatic event. It was disassembled over thirty years, piece by piece, each piece traded for a convenience that felt worth it at the time. This book is about who took what, who is using it, what they are using it for, and why the standard reassurances about your privacy are not true and have not been true for a long time.

The Wrong Fight: How the Climate Response Became the Climate Problem

The climate crisis is real. The policy response to it has been captured by the same industries that produced it, repackaged as green, and used to justify a transfer of wealth from ordinary people to the entities best positioned to profit from the transition. Energy poverty for working families. Regulatory frameworks written by the regulated. Carbon markets that pay polluters. Subsidies that flow to whoever has the lobbying budget rather than to whatever would actually reduce emissions. This book accepts the science and indicts the response. It is the book that the climate-denial left and the climate-action right both need and that neither side of the standard debate is willing to write.

The Quiet War: How America's Adversaries Attack Without Firing a Shot

The standard story about America's external threats is military: armies, missiles, alliances, the strategic competition that fills defense budgets and think tank reports. The story misses where the actual damage is happening. America's adversaries figured out decades ago that direct military confrontation with the United States is a losing proposition and that the more efficient path runs through covert operations, information campaigns, infrastructure compromise, financial penetration, and the patient cultivation of American divisions that the adversary did not create but is happy to amplify. This book traces the operations specifically: who is running them, what they are designed to accomplish, what they have already accomplished, and why the conventional military framing of foreign threats is leaving the actual war largely undefended.

The Dumbing Down: How American Schools Stopped Teaching Children to Think

American education stopped trying to develop independent thinkers and started trying to produce measurable outputs on standardized assessments. The shift was gradual, well-intentioned, driven by accountability politics that wanted to know whether teachers and schools were doing their jobs. The cost of that legibility was the unmeasurable thing the schools were supposed to be developing: the capacity for sustained reasoning, original argument, productive struggle with hard problems, the tolerance for ambiguity that genuine intellectual work requires. Two generations have now passed through this system. They can pass tests. They cannot reason. The book traces how the substitution happened, who benefited, and why the arrival of AI found an institution already oriented toward producing exactly the kind of student that AI dependency requires.

The Pattern: How the Enemies of You Work Together

The enemies named across this series are not parallel items on a list. They are a system. Cognitive erosion makes civic collapse possible. Civic collapse creates the conditions for kleptocratic capture. Kleptocratic capture funds the manufactured fear that legitimizes the surveillance state. The surveillance state runs on the educational system that produced citizens who cannot evaluate what is being done to them. Each enemy reinforces the others. None of them can be addressed in isolation. This book is the synthesis: how the system operates as a system, why the standard frame of fix-this-one-problem is itself part of the problem, and what counter-strategy looks like for someone who can finally see the whole shape of the attack.

The Debt Trap: How the Financial System Was Designed to Extract From You

Student loans that cannot be discharged in bankruptcy. Credit cards engineered to keep balances revolving. Mortgages structured so the first ten years of payments are mostly interest. Buy-now-pay-later services that have re-engineered impulse purchasing to operate on an installment basis. Auto loans that now run seven years and underwater within twelve months. Each financial product looks like a service. Each one is a specific design choice about who pays whom over time, and the design has consistently moved in the same direction. This book traces the architecture of consumer debt as a wealth extraction system, names the policies and corporate decisions that built it, and explains why the standard personal-responsibility framing is the cover story that lets the system continue.

The Sick Industry: How American Medicine Profits From Keeping You Sick

The American healthcare system spends more per capita than any other developed nation and produces worse outcomes on most measures that matter. The reason is structural. Chronic illness is more profitable than cure. Symptom management is more profitable than prevention. The food industry produces the conditions that the pharmaceutical industry then medicates. The hospital system bills by procedure, not by health. The medical research apparatus is funded primarily by entities with financial interests in particular conclusions. This book documents the architecture of medical extraction, names the specific incentive structures that produce it, and explains why the conversation about fixing healthcare has been confined to the question of who pays rather than what is being paid for.

The Gambling Machine: How America Made Predatory Gambling the Default

In 2018, sports betting was illegal in nearly every U.S. state. By 2024, it was legal and aggressively advertised in most of them. The expansion was not driven by public demand. It was driven by industry lobbying that succeeded because the public attention was on other issues. The new gambling environment is engineered with the full machinery of behavioral psychology: variable rewards, push notifications, free credits that require deposits, in-game betting that runs faster than judgment can keep up with. The financial outcomes are predictable and documented. The social outcomes are accumulating. This book traces how the legalization happened, who profited, and what is now being done to the people the new system has captured.

The Loneliness Engine: How American Life Was Structured to Isolate You

The third places where Americans used to encounter each other are gone. Bowling leagues, fraternal organizations, churches, neighborhood bars, civic clubs, parent-teacher associations: all measurably smaller, in many cases by orders of magnitude, than they were thirty years ago. The replacements are commercial products that provide the appearance of connection while delivering its opposite. This book documents the destruction of the institutions that made American social life functional, names the economic and policy forces that did the destroying, and traces the consequences for mental health, civic participation, and the basic human capacity to be known by other people.

The Theft of Childhood: How American Kids Stopped Becoming Adults

Children spend more time on screens than in any previous generation, less time outdoors than any previous generation, and reach standard milestones of independence later than any previous generation. The teen mental health collapse that accelerated after 2012 is not mysterious. The mechanism is documented. Phone-based childhood, helicopter parenting, the elimination of unsupervised play, the medicalization of normal developmental difficulty, and the school system's drift toward credentials over capacity have produced a generation that is anxious, fragile, and structurally unprepared for adulthood. This book names what was taken, who took it, and what would have to change for the next generation to get a different result.

Books by Richard Lowe

See books by Richard Lowe at

https://masterofworlds.com

Get free publishing insights and industry updates at

https://thewritingking.substack.com

For ghostwriting and book coaching services see

https://thewritingking.com

Index

IRS Form 990 (OpenAI), 147

J

journalism
    AI displacement of, 13, 70, 73,
        210–212, 218, 268, 282
    investigative, 211, 218
    local newspapers, collapse of,
        211, 218
Judge, Mike, 97
    Idiocracy, 24, 97

K

Kahneman, Daniel, 44
Keyes, Daniel, 47
    Flowers for Algernon, 47
Kruger, Justin, 50–51, 56
    Dunning-Kruger effect, 50–51,
        56
Kubrick, Stanley, 67
    2001: A Space Odyssey, 67

L

large language models, 46, 62, 71,
    82, 264
Liu, Jenny, 17, 29, 93
logic vulnerability (programming),
    64, 66

M

Marvin the Paranoid Android, 231
McKay, Adam, 214
    Don't Look Up, 214
memory
    externalized, 23, 42

Google effect, 17, 29, 93
    working, 30, 42, 104, 178, 268,
        272
Mentat (Dune), 129–130, 271
Microsoft, 115, 142
Milgram, Stanley, 76–77
misinformation, AI-generated, 145,
    209–210, 213, 220, 282

N

Newport, Cal, 95
    Deep Work, 95
Niccol, Andrew, 23, 190
    Anon, 23
    Gattaca, 190–191
No Child Left Behind Act (2001),
    123
novel arrives, when (limits of AI),
    199
Nvidia, 115, 142

O

open source AI, 144–145
OpenAI, 115, 142, 147–148
    IRS Form 990 mission
        revision, 147
    Pentagon contract, 142
original synthesis, 43, 104
Oshii, Mamoru, 289
    Ghost in the Shell, 23, 289
Overton window, 157, 160

P

pattern recognition, 58, 74, 171,
    197

Works Cited

Adams, Douglas. *The Hitchhiker's Guide to the Galaxy*. Pan Books, 1979.

Anthropic. "Acceptable Use Policy." Public statements and reporting, 2024–2026.

Bradbury, Ray. *Fahrenheit 451*. Ballantine Books, 1953.

Carr, Nicholas. *The Shallows: What the Internet Is Doing to Our Brains*. W. W. Norton, 2010.

Department of Defense. "Directive 3000.09: Autonomy in Weapon Systems." 2012, updated 2023.

Dunning, David, and Justin Kruger. "Unskilled and Unaware of It." *Journal of Personality and Social Psychology*, 1999.

Garland, Alex, dir. *Ex Machina*. A24, 2014.

Handshake. Job market data on entry-level positions for college graduates, 2024–2026.

Herbert, Frank. *Dune*. Chilton Books, 1965.

Indeed. Job posting data on programmer and software engineer roles, 2024–2026.

IRS. Form 990 filings for OpenAI Inc., 2018–2024.

Judge, Mike, dir. *Idiocracy*. 20th Century Fox, 2006.

Kahneman, Daniel. *Thinking, Fast and Slow*. Farrar, Straus and Giroux, 2011.

Keyes, Daniel. *Flowers for Algernon*. Harcourt, Brace & World, 1966.

Kubrick, Stanley, dir. *2001: A Space Odyssey*. Metro-Goldwyn-Mayer, 1968.

McKay, Adam, dir. *Don't Look Up*. Netflix, 2021.

Milgram, Stanley. "Behavioral Study of Obedience." *Journal of Abnormal and Social Psychology*, 1963.

Newport, Cal. *Deep Work: Rules for Focused Success in a Distracted World*. Grand Central, 2016.

Niccol, Andrew, dir. *Anon*. Netflix, 2018.

Niccol, Andrew, dir. *Gattaca*. Columbia Pictures, 1997.

Northwestern Medill School of Journalism. *State of Local News* report, 2024.

Oshii, Mamoru, dir. *Ghost in the Shell*. Production I.G, 1995.

Postman, Neil. *Amusing Ourselves to Death: Public Discourse in the Age of Show Business*. Penguin, 1985.

Publishers Weekly. Coverage of the AI publishing market and editorial workflows, 2023–2026.

Ryan, Thomas J. *The Adolescence of P-1*. Macmillan, 1977.

Sargent, Joseph, dir. *Colossus: The Forbin Project*. Universal, 1970.

Sparrow, Betsy, Jenny Liu, and Daniel M. Wegner. "Google Effects on Memory: Cognitive Consequences of Having Information at Our Fingertips." *Science*, 2011.

Stanford Digital Economy Lab. Reports on AI productivity and labor market effects, 2023–2026.

Stanton, Andrew, dir. *Wall-E*. Pixar, 2008.

Stephenson, Neal. *The Diamond Age: Or, A Young Lady's Illustrated Primer*. Bantam Spectra, 1995.